Be YOU

Tanya Waymire, A.C.C.

Clovercroft Publishing

Be YOU

© 2018 by Tanya Waymire

Published by Clovercroft Publishing, Franklin, Tennessee in association with OnFire Marketing.

Senior Editor: Tammy Kling

Assistant Editor: Tiarra Tompkins

Copy Edit by Robert Irvin

Cover Design by Jennifer McAlister

Interior Layout Design by Suzanne Lawing

Photography by Carmine LiDestri of Visual Image Photography

Printed in the United States of America

ISBN   Hardcover 978-1-945507-77-9
        Paperback 978-1945507-78-6

When you can silence yourself—enough—you just might hear God's purpose for you. Thank God His voice is louder than my doubts!

Vince and Jordan—you provided feedback along the way, and you encouraged me to stay the course. I love you both so much!

Tiarra and Tammy—you saw His intention for me before I did. You are visionaries and invaluable instruments to support others. Thank you for believing in me—and the resource my experiences could bring to others!

CONTENTS

INTRODUCTION

Be you.

There's a quote that says, "Be yourself—everybody else is taken." And it's really true.

I didn't write this book so I could receive accolades or notoriety. I wrote it for people who are seeking to grow personally and professionally. In other words, I wrote this book for you. If you are reading this, it is not an accident. You and I were meant to meet each other in the pages of this book. We were destined to connect.

What is the unanswered question that moved you to pick up this book?

Maybe there's some uncertainty about where you are in life, or perhaps you feel you've lost a piece of yourself and want to get it back. *Be YOU* was written to help you figure those things out.

If you flipped through the pages of this book before reading the Introduction, you may have noticed that *Be YOU* was designed differently than many of the books you have read before. If you would rather be a spectator and watch life from the sidelines, this book is not for you. However, if you desire to grow, expand your mind, and make an impact on this world, *Be YOU* will be an invaluable resource.

You can't grow as a human being if you aren't willing to do the work that will create change. Look inside yourself. Interact with the content. *Write in this book!* You will find space provided, in just the right places, so you can jot down your immediate thoughts after reading the content.

When our time together comes to an end, you will have a reference tool to revisit, one that will continue to help you as you move forward on your journey. If you find there are not enough lines to contain all your notes, use the side margins. The pages of this book are thicker than the average book, and that was done intentionally so you could write on the pages without fear of the ink bleeding through to the next page.

You are a complex, unique, interesting, and beautiful human being. Have you ever wondered why human is followed by the word *being*? Your journey through *Be You* will support your work toward becoming the person you are capable of being, and it will connect who you are with what you do professionally. When you can create a link between yourself, your teammates, and your workplace, the world becomes brighter, the flowers more fragrant, and victory even sweeter. In short, your life becomes a more enriching experience. It's really about being everything you were created to be.

I am excited to go on this journey with you. I have spent decades seeking and discovering some of the very things you want for your life. All my years of searching have led me to write this book, where our paths now intersect.

I used to define myself by my career until I realized that it didn't matter how much success I had if I was not fulfilled. Success by itself is never enough to satisfy your soul, and becoming aware of that fact changed my life.

I discovered that fulfillment came when I was able to help people who did not know what they wanted to do professionally. Satisfaction came when those who trusted me to guide them accomplished their goals. It wasn't my own success that brought joy to my heart; it came by helping *others* achieve victory for themselves.

I have hired, trained, and mentored a multitude of people over the last twenty-three years.

My teams have generated well more than $100 million in revenue for the corporations I have worked with. Outside of this, I have earned my certification as an Erickson Certified Professional Coach. I own and operate a coaching and speaking practice ded-

> Expertise in life comes from being willing to try, fail, and try again.

icated to supporting people and companies in their desire to become more. I am a member of the International Coach Federation, a highly respected organization with clear ethical standards and practices. I have also earned the right to be recognized at the Associate Coach Credit Level.

However, having all those credentials does not make me an expert at life. Expertise in life comes from being willing to try, fail, and try again.

We are all in this together, and I hope the training I have been through exemplifies my commitment to being the best I can be. I want to help others be the best they can be, and I'll do whatever it takes to make that happen.

What would you change, add, or delete from your life in order to be the best you possible? Why did you choose to work where you do—to "do" the work that is part of that role? This is a book that's going to make you think about those questions and hopefully help you answer them. It's my desire to help guide you through this journey of becoming the best you that you can be. To become a version of yourself that lives your best life possible. Life is short. You deserve to have joy in your life, and a balance that brings peace to your soul. You deserve to truly be *you*.

CULTURE

CHAPTER 1

BUILD HIGH, BUY LOW

What is the fundamental reason for growth? No matter what business you're in, growth requires getting out of your comfort zone and investing in something. You may invest your time or your money, but you *will* invest.

I am not a stocks or trading guru, but there is one precious commodity I know every business must have in order to operate: people. People fuel growth. And in order to grow people, you've got to invest.

People cause companies to grow, not the other way around. Great people are at the core of every customer experience that's gone right and every excellent delivery process. Nothing happens in a great culture without a team of excellent humans banding together toward a common goal.

People are the foundation of families, relationships, and most certainly every business on this planet. It is people who make the machine of business run. Despite this, many companies forget to invest in the people side of the business. Some companies unintentionally focus on building the processes and systems and neglect to nurture and build teams.

The Power of Teams

The strength and commitment of your team is one of the biggest contributing factors to your success . . . or lack thereof. Teams are the fuel for positive results. Teams run your culture and impact your clients. One individual will never be able to impact results on a process or system as much as a team will.

So how do you ensure your people feel inspired and motivated to perform at their best? As a leader, it is crucial to understand that this level of success is a combination of commitment, candor, and communication between you and your team that creates an environment of success.

I named this chapter for a purpose, so it would probably help if I gave some insight into what "Build" and "Buy" represent. "Build" represents developing a team member who is in your fold—one who is ready to be promoted. "Buy" means that you look outside your company to find new talent. Therefore, "Build High" means to promote from within, and "Buy Low" means to bring in new talent at an entry level. This is a theory I have watched many leaders struggle with, and that is primarily due to the different ways they view team members and new hires. What do I mean?

Let's say you're in buy mode, and you're looking outside the company for new talent. As you consider someone for a higher role in your company, you examine and acknowledge the positive traits that person would bring with them. You notice their performance in their current job and how well they communicate and work with others. Now, let's say you hire this candidate. As time progresses, their challenges and areas of opportunity not only become apparent to you, they become what you acknowledge *first* when thinking about this person. (Decisions like this—hiring from the outside—come from leaders evaluating the positive in new candidates while still focusing on the challenges and possible growth for those in existing roles.)

Why do leaders make such decisions? There are a few reasons, and one is that it's human nature to love new things, and we love the honeymoon phase of a new relationship. What's not fun about new?

It's a time when there is a common connection, and you tend to see all the attributes of a person in a positive way. You begin to form a mental picture of them on your team as one making a positive impact. New is about adventure. Old is about forgiving mistakes, resilience, digging in, and overlooking flaws. A combination of both is great for solid and long-term relationships.

I'm in the engagement business, so I tend to see the joy of a new relationship, day after day! In our company, sales is a huge part of what we do because you can sell someone on value by being descriptive and knowledgeable about product—in our case, engagement rings. And it's a happy sale, too, because every customer who walks in is in the pre-honeymoon phase!

In business, it's often the same way.

To better illustrate this concept, let's create a story. Let's say you have a new candidate—we'll call him Jordan—and you're in the honeymoon phase of the business relationship. You offer Jordan the opportunity to join your team, and he accepts.

A few months pass, and Jordan has integrated into the team nicely. But you begin to notice challenges in his skills or behavior. They're not so severe that you consider him a poor fit, but obvious enough to keep an eye on. You train him in such a way that he fully understands his responsibilities and what it means to be a leader on your team. Jordan is aware that the training to prepare for a leadership role is extensive, and he is committed to the goal. At some point in his development, you begin to give him more responsibility on your team. But this phase uncovers even more challenges in skills or behavior, and you begin to focus your coaching and development around these things.

Unexpectedly, you have a leadership role open up. You hadn't anticipated that happening for at least a year, yet here you are. You assess your internal candidates and realize you don't have anyone ready to take on this position. In fact, that is the position you were training Jordan for, but he is not ready. You carefully consider all your options, and realize that you are going to need to look for outside talent—to Buy High.

You begin the interview process, and through that you find someone you believe is the perfect candidate. Let's call her Amanda. She has years of leadership experience and a bevy of awards indicating her effectiveness. When she speaks, her tone and presentation provoke you to listen. You feel you have struck the right chord with Amanda, that she will be a great leader. You make her the offer, and she accepts.

Before Amanda starts, you sit down with Jordan to explain why you felt compelled to find someone outside the company for the position. You walk him through where he is in his development, and the risk it would have been to promote him too soon. He says, "Sure, I understand." Yet the disappointment is visible on his face. He knew he was training for the long game, but by putting someone else in the role, it became an even longer one.

Now you have Amanda on board as your department manager. She is eager to begin, but your team is concerned. How could they not be? They know nothing about her, yet they are to report to her. You need to choose a team member to support Amanda's integration into the company. Ironically, the person you feel is the best fit for this role is Jordan. When you ask Jordan if he would be willing to do it, he says yes.

While that may have been a relief for you, Jordan feels quite the opposite.

When Jordan begins the task of transitioning Amanda into the company, he observes a few issues with her skills and behavior toward the team. Jordan shares that information with you, and though you appreciate him bringing his concerns forward, your gut is telling you Jordan is going to be critical of Amanda because she stepped into the role he had been working toward. You had never witnessed these issues with Amanda yourself, so you dismiss them.

A few months later you notice that the team is not bonding with, or responding well to, Amanda. Seeking answers, you set up individual discussions with each team member. The feedback you get is sterile or dismissive altogether. How could this be? How are they not seeing in Amanda the same positive qualities you saw?

In order to find the answers to these questions, you meet with one of your most experienced and loyal team members, Melissa. She tells you Amanda does not project the values that characterize the company's culture, and when she is given a task to complete she does not follow company guidelines. Instead, Amanda makes up her own processes, which she claims are better.

You find yourself surprised by the information Melissa shared with you, especially since Melissa is typically the first one to step in and correct that sort of behavior. When you ask Melissa why she has not stepped in with Amanda, she informs you she has tried.

She sighs. "Amanda lacks listening skills," Melissa says. "She speaks over me, or cuts me off altogether, anytime I try to talk to her. She won't even stop what she is doing so we can have a conversation. I can't help someone who has no desire to be helped or simply believes they do not need any help."

You thank Melissa for her candor, and consider your next move. You decide to talk with other team members to get their perspective before determining what action you should take. In those discussions you discover the situation with Amanda is even worse than you feared. It appears her management style is in contradiction with the company culture. How could you have missed this in the interview process?

This question is easier to answer than you might imagine. Culture is a system of habits tied to values and purpose, but you have to live within that environment every day. The interview process cannot replicate that environment, so it is impossible to assess how someone will behave.

You set up a time to meet with Amanda and review her progress. During the meeting Amanda expresses that she feels things are going well. On paper, the results seem to support her view, but you know you must dig deeper

"Amanda, I am happy you have been delivering the results we need, but why are you not using our processes?" you ask.

Amanda expresses that she sees no value in gathering feedback first, and the way she is doing things is the only way she has been successful through her career. What you hadn't picked up on in the interview process is now becoming apparent. Amanda's positive results were driven independently and not inclusive of her team.

This is when you realize she is a myopic, or nearsighted, leader and her drive to succeed is fueled by her own desire for glory and recognition rather than the good of her team and the company. In the end, enriching the culture of the company has simply not been on her list of priorities.

You express to Amanda that the culture of the business is paramount to the synergy and momentum of the team. The people you have placed on her team are accustomed to having a voice and being involved in the outcome.

You decide to continue working with Amanda in an attempt to develop her into the kind of leader she should be. During this time, you receive a resignation notice from Jordan. When you sit with him to try and convince him to stay, you discover that not only is he disappointed at being passed over for the leadership role, he also feels that his training stopped once Amanda was hired. Additionally, he felt it was clear that Amanda's style of leadership was the way the company was planning to move forward, and that was contrary to the things he believed in.

What you hadn't noticed while spending so much time training Amanda was that you had abandoned Jordan and your commitment to him.

Even if Jordan did not resign, what do you think would happen to his attitude and demeanor? Would he still look forward to coming to work, and would he still have a desire to grow?

Buying High and dismissing internal opportunities will have a ripple effect. I realize there are times you must go outside of your company to find the right person, but if you have to Buy High more often than Build High, then you need to look at your processes for developing others.

Let's go back to the moment when the role for department manager first became available. Let's say that instead of immediately looking for outside talent, you take a closer look at Jordan's progress. What challenges does Jordan have that would influence you to look for talent outside the company? You find that he has two primary challenges. First, he has difficulty transitioning into a leadership role, and recognizing the line between being a team member and a team leader. Second, when making decisions he doesn't always do so from a leadership mind-set.

Ideally, you would love to have a few more months to prepare him. He is a great fit with the culture, an excellent collaborator, and is focused on exceeding expectations. Yes, he has challenges, but you know he will overcome them. You discuss the upcoming opening with Jordan. You ask him, if he were in your position, why he would want to promote him into a position of leadership.

"I work hard, and I want the team to win," he says confidently. "I have been working on the perceptions of others to see me as a leader and not a peer. I support your direction, and we trust one another. The team trusts me, and I trust them."

You ask Jordan, if he were promoted today, what he would struggle with, and why.

Jordan pauses, considers the question, then looks you in the eye and says, "I don't know all of the operational processes yet, but I know who to call if I get stuck."

You share your own observations with Jordan, and he admits

he was unaware of some of them. He agrees that they are valid and commits to changing.

If your supervisor asked you a similar question, what might those challenges be for you? Take a moment to think about it and make notes below.

_____

_____

_____

_____

_____

You promote Jordan and share the news with the team. All your team members are elated. Even though you had not shared with everyone that the current manager was leaving, somehow they knew. They were concerned about whom the replacement would be, and on hearing it would be Jordan, they are relieved. The team had been consistently successful, and Jordan's transition into management did not slow them down. As time passes, the challenges you and Jordan discussed become less obvious. Though you still commit time to Jordan's development, you actually have more time now to help others.

When you Build High, you protect your culture and show others there is opportunity to grow within your fold.

Promoting from within has much lower risk than Buying High, even if the external candidate has an amazing track record. Finding a candidate through the interview process who is a good fit with your culture is difficult at best, yet it is fundamentally critical to the sustained success of your company. Therefore, finding an outside candidate should be a Buy Low (in responsibility) if at all possible. That way the new hire has time to learn the culture and the opportunity to adapt to it.

There will be times when you Buy Low with a plan to fast track a new hire's growth.

Rather than it being a year or longer before they are ready to assume more responsibility, you create a road map that will enable the new hire to move to the next step in six months. Those six months provide sufficient observation time for you, as the leader, to see if the new person weaves into the fabric of your culture. It will also allow time for them to move through the Storming phase focused solely on their growth, and to acclimate themselves to the culture. Let's say your new hire joined your company soon after Jordan was promoted. You may assign Jordan the task of acclimating the new person. Jordan is excited about his promotion and his new role within the company, and his enthusiasm projects onto the new hire. Your new hire feels they made the right choice to join your company, and seeing that Jordan was promoted from within confirms his or her feelings.

So the moral of the story is to promote from within—unless you absolutely cannot. Build High and Buy Low will always be the lowest risk investment when it comes to people. As a leader, you've got to be committed to developing others and yourself. The first place great leadership starts is within. Even if your path isn't to take on a leadership title, understanding how these pieces come together will support your role within a team. You may need to be the Melissa who can see what others are missing.

> The first place great leadership starts is within.

And if you aren't involved in hiring people, there's a lot to learn from this thought process, because you will be the one being hired.

Develop yourself as a leader in all you do.

"Teamwork is the ability to work together toward a common vision."

—Andrew Carnegie

CHAPTER 2

THE KEYS OF CULTURE

What kind of culture do you work in? Ultimately, culture is all about the people, being focused on one general mission and environment, and working toward common goals.

_____

_____

_____

_____

_____

I've been involved with several companies where there has been a huge difference between what leaders believe their culture to be and what is truly being lived every day. Often, I think that leaders in such companies are seeking a silver bullet, a small tweak, or minor adjustments that will suddenly and magically turn everything around. The truth is that there is no quick fix, but there are a few key things that can be done that will work.

I like to use keys as an analogy, because we all use keys to enter the most valuable spaces we own. Whether it be your home, car, or office, we all use specific keys to access these places. Have you ever misplaced your keys? Stressful, right?

My son is adamant that he puts his keys and wallet in the same place every time he comes home. He still finds himself hunting for his keys, often. We've suggested to him that he put his keys on the key hook, but he insists that isn't necessary because he always puts his keys in the same place. Can you see the irony in that? Though we can visibly see he isn't putting them in the same place, he remains unconvinced. Until he sees for himself that there is a problem, he is unlikely to change this behavior.

The same kind of irony applies to the way many organizations view their culture. At an executive level, there may be the belief that the company culture is understood and practiced throughout all departments and locations. In some cases this perception may be correct, but in other cases it simply isn't. How can you tell if the perceived culture in your workplace is a reality? You ask. Taking the time to ask how your people view the company's culture is healthy. Do they understand and identify with the culture as it has been presented to them by management? Asking these type of questions and finding the answers is a healthy activity for any company.

> If your company is truly positioning itself to be sustainable for generations to come, then you understand that the culture is going to shift and change over time.

The workforce continues to change, and it is now common to see an age range from sixteen to seventy years old in many companies. With these and other challenges, maintaining a great culture can be difficult and needs to be monitored consistently. If your company is truly positioning itself to be sustainable for generations to come, then you understand that the culture is going to shift and change over time. This does not mean that your culture is going to turn on its head. It means that the identity of some of your keys may get a facelift. (There I go with the keys analogy again.) Let me share a simple framework that can be used to support your culture today and how it will continue to be a relevant structure for as long as you choose.

Imagine your culture represented on a key ring. You can have as many keys as you want, but you can have no less than three. Those three keys should represent the following:

> **Key A** – Purpose; or, The "Why"
>
> **Key B** – Core Values
>
> **Key C** – The How

Though these keys are labeled, they are equally important, and they cannot be separated. You can have more than these three keys, but more is not always better.

The three keys are all on the same ring. The key ring represents the company, the employees, and the community you are in. The keys protect the valuable and the key ring is the tight circle that keeps the keys together.

When you create your keys, remember that each key must align with the key ring in order to be sustainable. How can the key ring represent the company, its employees, and the community? It is because a healthy, thriving culture understands that all three are intertwined. Technology has advanced, and information and our availability to others is constant. Just as people will check their work email from home, the same people will respond to a text from a loved one or friend while at work. This is the new normal. How does your community intertwine? Whatever your business or service, it has an impact in your community. The way in which you serve the community will play a key role in whether your business thrives.

In the 1990s organizations were trying to define sustainability in their businesses. Things quickly got complicated until John Elkington created a simple and easy-to-understand model. In order for businesses to be sustainable, Elkington said, they must work toward a healthy triple bottom line (Hindle 2012). What is a triple bottom line? People, planet, and profit. These three must be valued and measured consistently for a business to thrive long-term. The triple bottom line relates to culture in this way:

> **People**—The Employees
>
> **Planet**—The Community You Operate In and Impact
>
> **Profit**—The Company's Gained Revenue

Using the keys and key ring analogy, let's take a look at what the keys could represent. Let's start with Key A, Purpose. As a company, why do you do what you do? Why do your team members believe in what they do? How do you support the community with your purpose? With those questions in mind, allow me to provide an example.

Key A: Purpose

We see a gap in the quality of product being offered. As companies work to cut costs, it becomes evident they are also cutting the quality being given to the customer. We believe people want a product they can trust, a product they can be proud of having purchased. So, rather than cutting quality along with costs, we want to find a way to control costs while still providing a high-quality product. Our team members are innovative, brilliant, and solution-focused people who share the vision that our customers deserve to get what they are paying for—and nothing less.

Note: In the Purpose outlined above, there is a hint at some of the Core Values that Key B represents.

What is the purpose within your culture?

_____

_____

_____

_____

Key B: Core Values

1) **Be Authentic.** Who you are is unique to you. Through authenticity ideas are born. Through your candor challenges are identified.

2) **Be Solution-Focused.** There is no value in dwelling on a problem. Determine the cause and then work toward the best possible solutions. Even if you helped create the problem, being a part of the solution shows strength in adversity.

3) **Be Humble.** Accept that no one is perfect, including yourself. Work to become the best version of yourself, and support your teammates. Be quick to listen and slow to speak. A humble person appreciates the value in others. This person is self-aware and self-accountable.

4) **Be Innovative.** Find new solutions and new ways of doing things rather than doing things a certain way because that is how they have always been done. Be creative, come up with new ideas, and execute on those ideas.

This is a relatively short list of core values, and it's a good idea to not try to come up with too many. You should be able to keep your list to no more than six. You can create more, but doing so will only make things more difficult to manage and implement. I have seen companies list as many as sixteen core values. While that may look good on paper, your team members will not be able to easily remember them all, let alone put them all into practice.

Ultimately, your purpose and core values are just words on paper—unless you and your team members actually live them.

What are the Core Values of your culture? If this doesn't align with what you want them to be, what *do* you want them to be?

_____

_____

_____

_____

_____

Key C: The How

1) **Hiring**. As some of the most celebrated architects of culture will tell you, it all starts with who you allow to be on your team. The selection process for a spot on your team shouldn't be "short and sweet." How many people should be involved in the interview of a potential candidate? How do you determine who interviews first and last? What are the pre-hire tools you are using that will help you identify the attributes you want in a candidate? There are many different approaches to filtering potential hires, and none of them are foolproof. Today's candidates can be well-scripted and know what you intend to ask. How quickly are they responding to your question? If they are hardly letting you finish before they start to speak, or even worse, begin to answer before you finish, that is a red flag. This person is showing a lack of active listening, and most likely lacks humility.

Ask questions that catch candidates off guard. They've likely interviewed at other places and may have a programmed response to mainstream queries. Realizing there are laws around what you can and cannot ask someone, you might ask, "If you had an unexpected day off, and could do anything you wanted, what would you do?" If the response is something having to do with the outdoors, you might follow up with, "Let's say it's raining on that day. Now what do you do with that time?"

Asking questions off the normal script will provide insight into who a person is and how they respond to challenges. These sorts of questions can also give you clues to a person's perspective. Since being solution-focused is one of your core values, did they offer up other ideas, or did they resign themselves and say, "Well, I guess I would just stay inside then."

You may love a candidate, but what do your second and third interviewers think? There will be times when you all unanimously agree on a candidate, and the hiring decision is an easy one. Other candidates will create conversation around the perceived positives and possible challenges. During those times remember to use your core values as your compass. A potential candidate must possess, or be capable of possessing, all of them.

I realize the thoughts that might be going through your head. These could include something like this: "We're shorthanded. I don't have the luxury of taking a long time to make a hiring decision. I will miss out on quality candidates if I don't act quickly."

This perspective will land you the wrong people, folks who will not only dilute your culture but could very well poison it. If you are shorthanded, work through the pain until you have the right person to fill the open position. The short-term pain will be quickly forgotten, but a wrong hire can be painful in the long run.

Even if you have a great hiring process in place, a poor hiring decision can still take place. You could hire someone who is humble, authentic, solution-focused, and shows the ability to be innovative. After they join the team, however, you may find that their desire to exhibit those values, and their ability to live them, do not align. For any number of reasons a change may need to be made. Then what?

2) **Coaching**. Just as you expect your team members to live the core values of the company, as a leader you must live them as well. If a new hire is struggling to adapt to the culture, have a conversation with them. Share your concerns, and have solutions ready to present to them. Be sure to collaborate with the new team member on other possible solutions. If you are a humble leader, your candor will be received in a positive way. Don't shy away from these conversations! If you feel one of your team members is struggling, I can assure you they feel what you are seeing. Having that conversation can be life-changing for them. You will likely start to see progress almost immediately.

If you have the conversations but do not see improvement, you should schedule follow-up conversations where the team member can update you on their progress. If they have indeed made progress, celebrate it. If they share information that is not authentic, call them on it. Establish a clear timeline for their improvement, and hold them accountable. Be sure you are giving them all the resources necessary to adapt and be an integral part of the team. Clarify what will happen if they aren't able or willing to adapt within that time frame. One of the options may be a role transition to a new position you believe would be a better fit for their skills, or you may suggest they be prepared to find a position outside your company.

That may sound harsh, but if you don't begin to see improvement quickly, and the team member has found ways to justify their lack of adaptation, you must be consistent in what is required to maintain a role on your team. Unless you have limitless payroll (and how many companies have that?!), each of your positions are critical to the success of the team and organization. Treat them as such. Each person must exemplify the culture.

3) **Communication**. To properly maintain your culture, you must communicate well with your team, and communicate often.

Any changes, challenges, or wins should be shared as quickly as possible, and throughout your company. How you and your team communicate is a direct reflection of your culture. Be aware of the methods you use to communicate. People tend to have habits around how they share information. There are those who speak positive in person, yet choose to email their frustrations. Other people may do the opposite. Neither approach is balanced or healthy.

The same can be said for people who choose phone calls or texting to communicate. Though some choices are made out of convenience, it is important to consider which form of communication is best for your message. All methods have their time and place when they are the best fit for the message. The key is to communicate.

4) **Encourage and Support Community.** Do you have a budget set aside to give back to your community? What about volunteering opportunities for you or your team members? What are possible areas of service in your community that are important to your team and company? These are good questions to ask your team. Whatever their answers, encourage and support them. People tend to be moved to causes that are close to their heart. If they want to donate their time but are unsure how to get started, help them find out. Donating time and money should never be a requirement, but when you support those who want to serve, you bring tremendous value to their lives.

If your team is already in place and you have defined what you want your culture to be, will everyone on your team thrive in that environment? If you have a team that has been in place for a long time and you wish to enhance your culture, it's still possible to do so. The most effective way to do this is to include your team in the process. Being the leader, you will ultimately determine the direction you all move in, but you will find your team will be a resource of great ideas on what the values should be, how to define them, and how to ensure everyone lives by them.

Recreating a culture where one already exists isn't an overnight process. Unless you're starting your own company, it will not be easy to change an existing culture. Depending on the size of the team (and company) you are working with, you may want support from outside the company to help you through the change.

Take a moment to write down "The How" of integrating your Purpose and Core Values into your team/company.

_____

_____

_____

_____

_____

CHAPTER 3

BUILDING A BRAND

What's your personal and business brand? Every company has a brand whether its employees know it or not. When it comes to impacting the brand of a company, the person in front of the customer is the one with the most power. The way in which that team member deals with the customer will impact whether the customer will refer your company to others. The team member who deals directly with your customers is the face of your entire company and its reputation. Sound like a great deal of responsibility? It is. It is crucial you and your team understand this. Every interaction with a customer is a direct reflection of your brand.

Your organization either has a label, or it is an established brand. What is the difference? Both are defined by the thoughts and feelings that arise when

> The team member who deals directly with your customers is the face of your entire company and its reputation.

your customers think of you. If the same thoughts and feelings arise across a large number of people, you are a brand. You may be an established brand in one particular market or globally. It is possible to have a market brand, but be a label at the global level. If people have heard of you, but don't have any real understanding of how to feel about your company, then you are a label. A brand has depth and consistency; the company has impacted its customers in a meaningful way. A label? Not so much.

Here is an example that will help clarify this concept. If I handed you a glass of dark soda and asked you what soft drink it was, you wouldn't know from merely looking at it. Now, if you tasted that dark soda, and you quickly recognized the flavor, you might say, "It's a Dr. Pepper!" The flavor and delivery of that product is so consistent that you were able to identify it without being given the name in advance. That is because Dr. Pepper is clearly a brand—at least in Texas. Would someone on the other side of the world easily recognize it as well?

Does your company fit within a label or a brand? What do people say when asked about your company? How does that align with your desired perception?

_____

_____

_____

_____

_____

We are all customers of one company or another. Why do you frequent certain businesses? Is it because they're convenient or the least expensive? You frequent certain businesses because of the service you receive, the value that business offers, and how it makes you feel. What do your favorite businesses have that others don't?

They have a team of people who are committed to the same goals and the same core values. They know why their company exists and who they serve. There is unity in the organization. It has a functional culture.

Culture is a compilation of the company's values and goals, the values and goals of the employees, and a commitment to giving back to others and the community. A business that readily comes to mind when I think of a vibrant culture is Sprouts Farmers Market. Sprouts is a chain of grocery stores, and when you shop in these stores you feel everyone who works there truly understands the concepts presented in this book. They are passionate about what they are doing, and their products support the community. If you're not familiar with Sprouts, the grocer offers fresh, locally supplied produce and meats. Regardless of what Sprouts I go to, I have the same experience and leave feeling the same way. Let's take a look at their culture from the three different areas mentioned in chapter 2.

Here is a snapshot of the company's values (www.sprouts.com/about). You can find these posted on the wall at every store, and you can see them as you are checking out:

Sprouts Core Values: Our core values reflect what is truly important to us as an organization. More than just words, these values embody the culture and spirit of Sprouts.

Initiative = Opportunity

Delegation = Personal Growth

Empowerment = Agility

Transparency = Trust

Accountability = Results

Mutual Respect = Positive Environment

Collaboration = Teamwork

Innovation = Relevance

Recognition = Inspiration

Passion = Enthusiasm

Though there are several values listed, each is strong and simple to understand. They are values an employee can be proud to represent. On a personal level, each team member strives to live the same values, so there is perfect alignment.

Why do they do what they do? Well, let's take a look:

> At Sprouts, we believe healthy living is a journey and every meal is a choice. We love to inspire, educate, and empower every person to eat healthier and live a better life.

Again, this is an ideology every person can get behind. A person who prefers to not make healthy eating choices as often as possible is unlikely to want a job here. If someone doesn't believe what Sprouts believes, they would struggle to enjoy their work. Great employees, whether they realize it or not, typically work for companies they can and want to support. The company's products or services have a common denominator with the life of its employees.

Now, even if you have a great company and a culture that attracts the right employees, you still have to be in tune with your potential customers. When Sprouts decided to open for business, the owners thought about what their customers wanted. They wanted fresh produce and meat they could feel good about buying. Their customers did not want to navigate a grocery store the size of two football fields to buy what they need to feed their families. Take a look:

> Great employees, whether they realize it or not, typically work for companies they can and want to support.

Sprouts – A Healthy Grocery Store that Flips the Conventional Model

- Produce surrounded by a complete grocery offering
- Promote value everyday
- Differentiated assortment of high-quality, healthy foods:
  - Do not carry most national- branded CPG items
  - Fresh, natural and organic offering
  - High standard Private Label rooted in quality and taste
- Farmers market-inspired open store layout with low profile displays
- Convenient, small-box: 30k sq. ft.
- Friendly, engaged customer service, easy to shop environment

Nearly all Sprouts stores have a similar size and layout. Why? When you have to go into a store in a different location, a customer can easily find what they need. Quick, simple, and affordable. Since its launch in 2002, Sprouts has joined a larger organization and become publicly traded on NASDAQ—and it has not strayed from the original core values. It's no wonder Sprouts is one of the fastest growing retail chains in the country.

With rapid growth comes the risk of your culture/brand becoming diluted. An example comes to mind of a company that came into the Dallas/Fort Worth area and began opening locations very quickly. Jackie, a young college student, was hired for one of the first locations that opened. She loved it! The managers were motivating, the team positive, and she enjoyed the customers a great deal. Her best friend, Leigh, hearing how much she loved working there, decided to apply to be hired at the location that was just about to open near her house. She attended the job fair that was offered, and she was hired immediately.

Leigh's experience was nothing like her friend's. Communication was weak, schedules changed at the last minute, and training was nearly nonexistent. When she voiced her concerns to a manager, she was shut down and dismissed. The enthusiasm she had in join-ing the company quickly disappeared. Within a few months, Leigh chose to leave. How could their experiences be so different?

> The values, principles, and actions of store managers set the tone of a subculture.

Though the company has an over-arching culture, every location has a subculture. The values, principles, and actions of store managers set the tone of a subculture. In Leigh's case, those charged with leading the store had behaviors that did not align with the culture the fast-growing chain had built its brand on. It is likely that the levels of success at that location are not on par with neighboring stores that are operating in alignment with the overarching culture. How can I make this assumption?

I've spent years working in operations of corporations with mul-tiple stores. Regardless of the company, the same trends exist. Some locations consistently deliver the revenue expectations, while oth-ers are consistently inconsistent. The poor-performing locations have high turnover in leadership, a lack of buy-in from the teams, and challenges in building their customer base. Those same stores would blame their poor performances on extenuating circum-stances. Rarely have I heard leaders accept responsibility for lack-luster performance. I have heard things like, "The unemployment rate around my location is record high"; or, "Our product pricing is too high for the customer base we serve"; or, "People can't get approved for credit."

I realize there are circumstances out of direct control that impact results. However, it is usually low-performing leaders that generate low performing results. I have noticed that when there is a change in leadership, and someone with a drive to succeed takes over, things suddenly turn around. Without even a word, the economy improves, people have jobs, and the customers are suddenly able to get approved on credit.

To be fair, a low performing leader in one company can be a high performing leader in a different company. How? The person finds the right fit for what truly motivates them.

Look around at your own company culture. How can you become a stronger part of the team? Cultures are driven by people and the relationships and connections those people make. An individual employee is not a culture. A collective of employees working independently, yet together, toward common goals, creates the culture.

Some companies have cultures you simply might not fit into. If you applied for a role as a barista at Starbucks, you would likely find the environment quite different than if you applied for a retail sales position at Ralph Lauren. Different companies have different cultures, and those cultures are based on whatever type of brand message the company intends to convey.

Ever heard the saying "you can't fit a round peg in a square hole?" If you've never felt in alignment with your company culture, maybe there's a reason! Generally, a strong culture will identify those who don't fit fairly quickly. And that's OK! Cultures are like friendships, relationships, fraternities, or clubs. You wouldn't join a skydiving club if you hate heights, and you wouldn't join a culture that opposed your core needs or ideals either.

CHAPTER 4

EVOLVE OR DISSOLVE

If I were to ask you who the most important person in your company is, who would you say that person is? If you work in an organization with infrastructure that includes part-time employees all the way up to executives, it is likely you would say the CEO or company president. Given that there is only one CEO and lots of full-time and part-time team members, imagine a triangle with the CEO at the top point and full-time and part-time team members represented along the bottom line.

As you label these positions on the triangle below, fill in all the other positions and where they relate within the triangle.

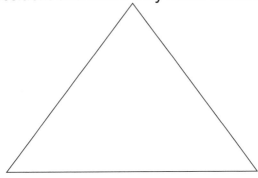

Now look at your triangle. How do you feel about it? What if I told you that this is an old school way of thinking? It is referred to as a top-down culture. It is a traditional method of pushing direction down to the people. It creates an environment of compliance because whether directives are understood or not, they are expected to be executed.

If your organization has a customer on the other end of your work, *the most important person can't be considered the person furthest from that customer.* The most important person in the company is the one closest to the customer, because it is that person who creates the experience for the people creating your revenue.

Now, this isn't to diminish your answer. The CEO or president—that person is vitally important. This is the person charged with making decisions and creating a plan that helps your company grow. The CEO is a vital part of the organization, and that role carries great responsibility. If the CEO makes a series of good decisions, your company thrives. If he or she make a series of bad ones, the company suffers.

Now take that same triangle, still labeled accordingly, and flip it so that the long line is at the top, and the point is at the bottom.

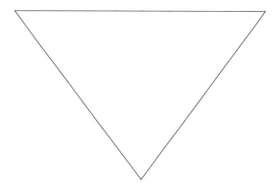

The most important people now are the team members who are in front of your customers. In this cultural model, when decisions need to be made, executives and company leaders seek information from all team members. They look to be sure that any changes that are being contemplated have a positive impact on the brand.

Good leaders understand the importance of getting the perspective of those on the front lines with the customers. When change is inevitable, company executives should meet with all team members to allow questions, thoughts, and concerns.

Though a change may still need to occur, everyone in the company will now understand why. Everyone can move forward with a sense of commitment rather than mere compliance. This is referred to as a bottom-up culture.

In a bottom-up culture, everyone is empowered to make decisions that impact the brand of the company and the customer's needs. If someone makes a decision and it is later discovered that this was not the best decision, the employee is not chastised for making that decision. They are appreciated for it because everyone on the team will benefit from learning how to handle things better the next time. This structure supports self-accountability and encourages people to have a voice. James C. Hunter wrote a great book called *The Servant*. I recommend picking it up; it illustrates this principle further.

Here is where the best brands turn things on their head, literally.

Remember that traditional triangle model flipped upside down? The long line is at the top and the single point is at the bottom. It may look odd, seeing the triangle upside down, but the old way of the point being at the top is not stable. But you may be thinking that the triangle cannot be stable while balanced on the single point, and you would be correct in that assumption.

So, flip the triangle back the way it was. Here is where the magic happens. Rather than all ideas and direction flowing down from the top of the triangle, the stream of valuable knowledge starts by *running upward from the bottom*. New ideas and feedback from customers begin to flow from your frontline team members up to those responsible for steering the company in the right direction. Many of those ideas will translate into company-wide changes. Here is what this model looks like:

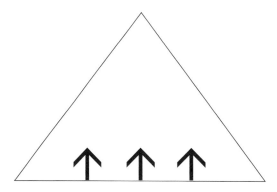

The leadership of the company designs and implements changes, gives credit to those from whom the original ideas came, and shares them with the entire company. This two-way flow of information creates an enlightened organization that understands the importance of encouraging feedback and implementing ideas that benefit the whole.

My career spans more than twenty years, and I have lived both the old-school model and the new generation model. I can quickly observe a team that is compliant, and I can discern a team that is committed. In the old school approach, it is rare to observe commitment from employees that is not fueled by compliance.

You might be asking yourself why it matters whether your people are compliant or committed. After all, things are getting done. And you're right, things are getting done, but they won't be done in the way

> Commitment is having a full understanding of the reason behind a change, and clarity on how long it may take to see full impact.

you expect if you only have team members who are complying. On the surface, there isn't a big difference between compliance and commitment, but that difference is significant to the change being sustainable. Commitment is compliance with a buy-in as to why it is being done and how it will benefit the company and team members.

Commitment is having a full understanding of the reason behind a change and clarity on how long it may take to see full impact. Commitment is gained when people are allowed to ask questions, provide feedback, and participate in the change.

Think of a time you were compliant, and compare it with a time you had full commitment to direction being given. What were the factors that created each?

_____

_____

_____

_____

_____

In every company there are times when this process has to be sidestepped. Such urgent adjustments come with an understanding that, due to an immediate need, the new direction has to be implemented immediately. Acknowledge and appreciate the support from all team members in understanding that that is not how you would have wanted to make things happen, and thank everyone for understanding.

How can you still get a commitment from your team members around these times?

After the new direction has been executed, ask for feedback from your people. Gather information from everyone affected by the change. Make sure the flow of feedback, along with suggested solutions, adjustments, and support systems, are all acknowledged. Once you've assessed all the feedback, make any necessary modifications to the change and credit those who supplied the important feedback.

When people in your company hear an executive thanking an employee by name for their great feedback, not only does this make them feel valued, these employees tend to feel a type of ownership in the company. Their idea will be implemented across the entire organization. Other team members take notice, and many will find inspiration in knowing ideas don't fall on deaf ears. I have seen only positive results from acknowledging others.

> I have seen only positive results from acknowledging others.

The opposite of this principle is also true. When a company squashes the ideas of its employees, they feel disrespected, devalued, and disconnected.

Think of a time when you gave credit to a team member for his or her great idea. What was the outcome?

_____

_____

_____

_____

_____

I saw a great example of this the other day. Papa John's Pizza has a commercial in which you see a young chef working through different styles of deep dish pizza pans. The narrator is sharing how this young chef wasn't OK with using just any pan to make the best pan pizza—he personally tested all the pans he could until he found the one he felt was worthy of holding a Papa John's deep dish pan pizza. His name was on the screen. He was given full credit for this. Only at that point in the commercial did Papa John, the owner and face of the company, emerge. He gave full and complete credit to this chef.

Conversely, I've observed great ideas shared from team members to direct supervisors who promised to share the idea up the chain. But by the time the idea reached the top of the chain, credit for it wasn't given to the originator. What's worse is that many times the credit was given to some mid-level manager who took it up the chain. Have you ever seen this occur? If you haven't, count yourself fortunate.

On the occasions that I have, the disappointment felt by the team member is obvious. In nearly every case of observing such things, I can only recall a couple of instances when the manager getting credit stepped up and clarified where the idea truly came from. Why is that? In the cases that I have seen, I don't believe it is because the managers want to slight the team member. I believe it's because they're concerned with backlash if they correct the company's leader.

Moving forward, how do you believe the team member who wasn't acknowledged is affected? Have you ever heard phrases such as "I'm just here to get a paycheck" or "It's only a job"? Complete disengagement is the usual response. If not addressed and corrected, this nearly always leads to the person leaving for another job.

> Usually people who share a great idea have the capacity to share many great ideas.

Usually, people who share a great idea have the capacity to share many great ideas. Imagine the momentum that old-school company could have gained from many great ideas from that person who chose to leave the company. You would have an organization that's capable of adapting to the changes in society. You would have a company that not only sustains its position in the market but would likely continue to thrive even in challenging economic times. This organization would not only attract business, it would also attract great talent. With more great talent would come even more great ideas that could improve the company.

How am I so sure such a company would attract great talent?

Just as customers share their experiences and make recommendations about your business, so do your employees. They share feedback with friends and family. When they are appreciated, acknowledged, and feel a responsibility in the overall success of the company, they speak of their work with enthusiasm. Even if there are challenges, the positive feedback regarding how important they feel is a referral to others. Those friends, very possibly unhappy in their current jobs, will likely remember how their friend feels within their role. I find that bright people tend to surround themselves with other bright people. When your company begins to hire people who were referred, trust is usually achieved much more quickly. The transition time from joining to performing is shorter. And the team member who recommended the new person feels ownership in the company in helping it be successful.

If you are a hiring manager, you probably recognize this already. The most successful teams I've been part of formed from referrals from other great team members. The synergy created served as momentum toward exceeding expectations. This creates a beautiful and positive snowball effect that supports the company's growth.

> Just as customers share their experiences and make recommendations about your business, so do your employees.

Let's go back to the team member in the old school model, the one whose idea was stolen. As a hiring manager, if you went to this person and asked them if there was anyone they could refer to work at your company, what do you think would happen? What kind of person, if anyone, might they recommend? Here's my insight.

My son is a college student, and he has a close group of friends with a wide network of people they spend time with. Since my son and his friends were in junior high, our home has been the gathering place for all of them to spend time together and relax. As they went from middle school to high school, these boys became part of our family. I treated all of them as my own.

They no longer arrive at our house every weekend, but when they do come over I love to hear how things are going for them. Every one of them has worked since high school; some full time and some part time, depending on their other responsibilities. And when they talk to me about their jobs, I can almost tell you how long they will work there.

The jobs they have left had a common theme. There was a lack of appreciation, unprofessional managers, and a general lack of communication. Within that core group of six friends, whenever one of them becomes unhappy with their job, they ask the others what they think of their jobs. What sort of feedback do you think they give?

Operate with a hierarchy that understands the significance of every team member and how they

> Operate with a hierarchy that understands the significance of every team member and how they impact your organization.

impact your organization. Your employees, and how they view your company, will have a direct impact on the perception your customers have of your company. If what your employees think about working in your organization concerns you, take a look at what they are communicating to others. What your employees express in words begins with how they feel. You may not be able to change how they feel, but you can change what made them feel that way. If there is negative feedback, don't be old school and reprimand the team member. Appreciate the information coming to light, and adjust accordingly.

It's not too late to evolve, because evolution is constant.

"Culture makes people understand each other better."
—PAULO COHELO

CHAPTER 5

TIME AND ENERGY

How much time and energy do you have to dedicate to the things that are important to you? Time is simple because we all have the same amount. No one has more than anyone else—unlike wealth or dollars or net worth.

Time is somewhat easy to discuss. Time is just twenty-four hours in a day. There are only sixty minutes in every hour. Time cannot be changed to represent twenty-five hours in a day or seventy minutes to an hour. It is consistent and unending. Energy, within a person, is much the same. Just as time is already laid out, I believe each human being is constructed with the same amount of energy as the next person. I believe this energy is consistent and unending, meaning it starts fresh with each new day. (I will elaborate, I promise.) It's important that we are able to see how time and energy are intertwined.

Think of someone you know who is always busy.

> It's important that we are able to see how time and energy are intertwined.

Watching this person, or hearing them speak about their day, exhausts you. Not only are they productive in their work, they go to their kid's sporting events, have dinner with friends, attend church on Sunday, volunteer for local causes, and take vacations in other countries. Have someone in mind? We all do.

Who came to mind? What is it about that person that made you think of them?

_____

_____

_____

_____

_____

I am going to let you in on my perspective of how they do it.

If you know me personally, then the person I described above probably made you think of me. I have been asked how I do as much as I do; I sometimes watch people get tired as I describe a schedule they deem impossible. After being asked this question so many times, I wanted to take a close look at how I do it. The consistent element I have found from one highly productive person to another is the use of energy. Like time, if you are given so many units of energy to spend, how you spend that energy is what truly matters. I am as deliberate as possible with my energy so I don't waste any of it on things that don't support those around me, my goals, or His purpose. By intentionally spending energy in areas that align with my values and deliberately not wasting it on things that don't, I appear to accomplish far more than others.

Today, I am better at being more deliberate than I was even two years ago. As I've gotten better at spending energy with purpose, it is because I've identified those situations in which I was spending it foolishly and then made a conscious decision to not give my energy to those things any longer.

When I wake up, I begin my day with no less than fifteen minutes of reflective time. During this time I don't check my phone, turn on my television, or even worry about what the weather is going to be. I make a cup of coffee, and I appreciate the day. Many times this fifteen-minute space finds me with someone on my heart. Sometimes, the time provides me with a specific intention to take away. When you quiet yourself enough, you are able to feel these intentions.

> When you quiet yourself enough, you are able to feel these intentions.

As I drive to work, I choose content that supports my positive, productive choices. Had someone been on my heart earlier, I reach out. If my time was met with silence, I may continue my ride to work in the same silence. Should I find it hard to be present in that silence, for whatever reason, I turn on an audio book to give my mind content to focus on.

Once my day at work has begun, I make myself available to others. If someone approaches me to have disruptive conversations, I kindly let them know that there has to be something better to talk about. If they continue down the other path, I let them know that I am not their audience, and I won't listen. I push them to the person the content is about. If they decide to not speak with that person about it, then it wasn't important to begin with.

When my day ends and I am on my way home, I briefly touch base with my family, and then I enjoy the ride home. I create a peaceful space while I drive, and I reflect on my day. Should a thought arise that I need to give attention to, I voice message it to myself. Once I'm home, I work on projects that support my personal growth and my family as a whole. I put my phone away, and I am fully present with my family to be productive. Whether I am listening to the events of their day, writing, or cooking, the energy I am spending brings me joy.

On my days off, I start the day the same way. I add in some productive time with my dogs, who always appreciate a long walk. After this, I spend my energy focused on tasks and projects that support my family and goals. They are full days. Nearly all of them include coaching clients, business planning for myself, and tackling the next steps to personal and family projects. (I am in this space, leaving many things out as they pertain to my actions. I spend time in prayer, at the gym, and on other errands as well.)

If you were able to realize more in a day, what are the things that would show up that you would bring into your day?

_____

_____

_____

_____

I am determined to spend my energy in ways that are productive and beneficial. Part of being able to do this means I had to identify my energy wasters. I have identified many and listed a number of them below. Your energy-wasters may be different than mine, but you will probably recognize a few.

Social Media: Between the notifications coming in and people asking if I saw something that someone else posted, it felt like I was viewing social media throughout my entire day. I turned the notifications off, and though it slowed some of the distraction, those distractions weren't removed as one of my biggest time and energy wasters until I deleted it from my phone. I look at social media for only a few minutes in the morning and a few in the evening, and only if I feel like it.

Traffic: I commute almost seventy miles a day. I see a lot of lovely drivers that enjoy hindering my ability to get to work in an efficient manner. OK, not really. But I will say that I used to allow myself to get frustrated. That frustration is spent energy. Now I use the drive time to listen to audio books that support my inner growth.

Analyzing the Choices of Others: I would wonder why someone did what they did. I would think of certain scenarios, then think of still others. This type of thinking depletes your energy. Now if such thoughts show up, I don't waste my energy analyzing them.

Judging Others: This is different than analyzing the choices of others, because analyzing is my trying to understand the reasoning someone used. Judging others is when I am disagreeing with another's decisions and consciously going through what would have been a better choice (as though I actually know better). I have taught myself to appreciate that people make the best possible decisions they can with the resources they have available. I applaud them for making a decision. If it is work related, I may ask how they reached the point they did and possibly brainstorm with that person other possible choices for next time. Lack of judgment encourages people to act.

> You cannot control whether you get mad or angry, but you have complete control over how long you are mad or angry.

Anger/Frustration: This eats your energy twice as quickly as any other waster, in my opinion. What's the value in it? Nothing productive that I have been able to discern. The mantra I created to move beyond this point is this: *You cannot control whether you get mad or angry, but you have complete control over how long you are mad or angry.* This is how I began to take back what is mine and stopped flushing my energy down the drain.

Worrying About Things I Cannot Control or Change: Boy, have I fed this energy waster through the years! I adopted a mantra that helped me move beyond this. It is from poet Maya Angelou (www.mayaangelou.com): "If you don't like something, change it. If you can't change it, change your attitude." My adaptation is this: If I don't like it, change it. If I can't change it, I have to change the way I think about it.

If you look at your energy and how you spend it, what are your biggest energy wasters? How might you remove those from your habits?

_____

_____

_____

_____

_____

Finally, let's give energy a unit count just to help illustrate my perspective. If we are all designed with one hundred units of energy that align with the twenty-four hours in a day, I estimate that I used to give no less than thirty to thirty-five of my units to waste. As I began discovering that I have a specific amount of energy allotted for each day, my waste was cut to less than ten. The shift in how I spend those units is evident to others.

Imagine yourself spending your one hundred units in the most productive, purposeful way you can. What happens?

_____

_____

_____

_____

_____

Most of the complications that distract us, causing us to waste our energy, are created by us. When you can teach yourself to starve those distractions, you'll notice the extra energy you now have. If you could accomplish anything you wanted, what would that be? How many units of energy would you need? Where can you move those units from?

LEADERSHIP

CHAPTER 6

HAVE YOU EVER BEEN FIRED?

If you've ever been downsized, let go, or fired, you're going to love this chapter.

Let's start with this: If a company is thriving, and they let you go only to hire someone else to take your place, then I don't believe you were fired. There are times when that perspective could be wrong. You see, firing someone implies they were let go for reasons other than their own choices. Firing feels like failure to the one being fired and to the one who has to do it.

I can only recall one instance when I actually had to fire someone. The company I worked for was undergoing a restructuring, and the labor budget had been drastically cut. In that particular case, I had to fire four people, and those people will forever be in my heart because firing them contradicted my core principles. When you're a leader, charged to protect and support a team, even firing one person can make you feel as though you're compromising the promise you made to that person when they were hired.

You might be asking yourself, "If I'm a leader, how in the world could I manage to effectively operate and not fire people?" That is a great question.

I have led thousands of people, and I made sure each and every one of them had all the support and tools they needed to be successful. I have trained hundreds of leaders to be transparent with their team members and to provide them clear action plans. I also trained them to revisit those plans on a regular basis so their team never had to wonder what was expected of them. Most leaders have had the experience of a team member asking if they were going to be fired. Here is the response every leader should give to that question:

"Absolutely not. I will give you all the tools and information you need to succeed. I will be here to support you anytime you need it. It is up to you to put in the work. It is up to you to put into practice all that we teach you. If you choose not to do that, I won't fire you, because you will be making a clear choice to let your position go."

I have had people ask that question, and many of them let their positions go. I believe the reason to be self-accountability, or rather the lack of it. *When a person refuses to hold themselves accountable for their decisions and actions, they cannot effectively perform their role—in any workplace.* What must be understood is that people who hold to that viewpoint will poison the culture of a business.

> Individuals who lack self-accountability tend to play the victim in nearly every situation.

These are the people who move around the team creating conversations about how unfair the managers are, how they hate their job, and so on. Individuals who lack self-accountability tend to play the victim in nearly every situation.

If you take any team and divide it up by high performers and low performers, you will see the biggest difference is the level of self-awareness and accountability each team member possesses.

Does this mean you should take all the low performers and let them go? No! It means you have genuine, open conversations that clarify what the team member is lacking, how they might change it, and what support you can provide to encourage it.

Some low performers have habit systems they brought with them from previous jobs or even from their upbringing. They don't know what they don't know. As you walk them through this conversation and the action plan that follows, you will begin to notice changes. Celebrate their progress and continue to support them. As time progresses, challenge them more. By doing this you will a positive impact on that person that will last a lifetime.

On your team, who can you support to turn the corner from low performance to self-accountable high performance? (Maybe it's even you!)

_____

_____

_____

_____

_____

Other low performers will resist change. These people are easy to spot because they make no progress whatsoever, even though you had the same conversation with them that you had with other low performers who turned things around. These are the individuals who will place the blame on anything and everything except themselves. There will always be some people in this world you cannot reach no matter how hard you try. They are comfortable in their habits and will eventually let their positions go. Even then, they will likely not accept responsibility.

I experienced the perfect example of this a few years ago with a jeweler we had hired. His supervisor had multiple conversations with him and gave him an excellent action plan to improve his performance. Despite all this, the jeweler continued to work on pieces he wasn't allowed to work on. He continued to create errors that had to be corrected by other jewelers. When the day came that we had to let him go, he kept saying he understood, and that "The holidays are over, and you only hired me for the holidays." I let him know, clearly, that we were going to have to hire someone to fill the role he was letting go. I let him know that he was not hired only for the holidays. I told him he was being let go because he chose to ignore all direction and had thus created hardships for others. Even after being told plainly why he was being let go, he left saying that we had only hired him for the holidays.

I cannot fathom why someone operates in this fashion. To not be responsible for one's own actions is not something I can relate to. Therefore, I can't shed much light on why some live in this way. I can, however, shed plenty of light on how to recognize it. Looking back on people I have hired who later chose to let their positions go, I found some red flags that one might see in the hiring process. As much as a leader wants to hire as perfectly as possible, there will still be people who do not work out. The key is to learn from those situations so you can avoid them in the future.

During the interview process, ask the types of questions that will draw out answers that reflect on self-accountability or the lack of it. For example, you may ask a candidate how many times they were late for work at their last job. Keep in mind that you are not looking for a specific number as much as you are setting up the follow-up question: "Why were you late that number of times?"

A self-accountable person will own up to the reasons. Someone who isn't will deflect responsibility to someone or something other than themselves. We all know someone who plays the blame game.

The third question should be something like, "If we were to hire you, how will you be sure that doesn't happen here?"

That is one example; I won't bore you with a series of them. I want to encourage you to decide what values you will not compromise on, and then determine how you can create interview questions that help identify a candidate who possesses them.

What are your uncompromising values that you expect a team member to have?

_____

_____

_____

_____

Write some sample interview questions that support these values.

_____

_____

_____

_____

If you have a team full of people who deflect responsibility, that lack of self-awareness is a thread in the fabric of your culture. It's got to be stopped, recalibrated, and a true leader must step in. A team that isn't accountable is easy to lead, and that's the good news. Normally a team without accountability just hasn't been led by a strong and intentional leader. *People want to be led.* They want to be accountable and successful. They desire to achieve big goals! How can you work to step in and create a more accountable team? Think on these things as they apply to you, your life, your business, and the culture you live and work in.

> Normally a team without accountability just hasn't been led by a strong and intentional leader.

How would you define your culture? This could be your workplace or the place you live. Yes, culture extends to the home.

_____

_____

_____

_____

CHAPTER 7

RUDOLPH AND THE ISLAND OF MISFITS

Chemistry is everything. It impacts culture, teams, and the way people interact in their quest for results. How does chemistry impact performance and lives?

Have you seen the animated movie *Rudolph the Red-Nosed Reindeer*? It's a holiday classic, and if you have children, you've probably seen it many times. In the movie, there is an island where toys that were made a little different, or were not right for the intended child, end up. Hence the name: The Island of Misfit Toys. Some toys on the island are sad, while others are happy.

Rudolph was considered a misfit at first. His red nose made him different, and others made fun of him. Yet when the time came, Santa knew exactly which reindeer he needed to pull his sleigh through the inclement weather. The very thing that had labeled Rudolph a misfit ended up being what qualified him to lead Santa's sleigh. When Rudolph used his bright nose to lead the sleigh and save Christmas for the children, the rest of the reindeer not only appreciated him, they accepted him completely. So, are you wondering why I'm talking about a reindeer with a bright nose and misfit toys? I bet you have a guess.

Every time you bring someone new to your team, that person's role isn't determined right away. I don't mean role as in the job they were hired to do, but the role as it pertains to the synergy on your team. Whether your team is large or small, when someone new enters the fold they are watched closely by your team. Your veteran team members will try to figure out why you hired the new person, what makes them worthy of joining the team, and how will they impact everyone else.

It would be simpler if they would simply ask the hiring manager these questions, but the reality is most won't. Even if they do ask, their perspective may well be different from those who did the hiring. They are in the trenches, if you will, of the daily operations of your business, and that makes their viewpoint a little different.

The less turnover you have with your team, the more uncomfortable it can be for someone new to try and integrate. I don't believe it's because your seasoned team wants to squeeze them out. It's because the team has worked together for a long time and has reached a master's degree level, so to speak, in their relationships with one another. It would be like going to a class reunion and being the only person in attendance who didn't grow up with everyone else.

Think about your team dynamic. How might a new person trying to integrate perceive your team members?

_____

_____

_____

_____

_____

Given the natural inclination for these things to occur, I encourage you to partner a new hire with a team member who has respect among the group and can help soften the integration period. The buddy should be the person on the team who is most like-minded with the new hire. By sharing common ground, or behavior style, it is easier for the new person to be more authentic (first gateway to a master's). Let me address something honestly: I hate to keep referring to the new team member as the "new hire" or "new person." So let's call this person Misty, and for the purpose of our illustration, let's call her buddy Susan.

Susan takes the time to answer any questions Misty may have. She introduces Misty to other team members. She gets to know more about Misty and how she will fold into the team. Granted, these are assumptions on Susan's part, but as a senior on the team, she is familiar with the process. There was a time Susan was new, when she was in Misty's shoes. Because of that, she will have empathy and try to support Misty as she acclimates.

In time, Misty's authenticity and transparency begin to reveal how she thinks, what her initial information filters are, and where she fits within the team. It is there, in that raw space of acclimation, that the culture fit begins. Once she's been on board for a few weeks, the new-person jitters will fade, thus allowing her to respond and react genuinely. Does her behavior throw up green or red flags? Are her initial filters positive or negative? What is the general and unsolicited feedback of her teammates?

In Misty's case, they are nearly all green; the team feedback is positive. Misty not only folds into the team quickly, her job performance mirrors that of your veterans. She's a great hire and a great fit. If only hiring would work out so well every time.

There's a saying that in order to appreciate a great day, you must experience a bad one. The same can be said for bringing new people into your fold. Of the thousands of people I have hired, I can recall some pretty bad hiring decisions. As the years have turned into decades, the percentage of bad hires has certainly decreased, but no one has a perfect batting average, even as much as we strive for one.

When I look back on those who were misfits, there isn't a common thread that ties them together. I recall having concerns in the interview process, but they weren't necessarily big concerns. Now I could say that you should pass on every candidate for which a flag comes up, but I promise you that if you do that you will miss out on some great talent. Just as I remember the flags with the misfits, I also remember flags that came with some of the greatest additions I ever placed on a team. What's the difference?

The difference can be narrow, but the defining difference between the great ones and the misfits is a partnership in change. The great hires showed humility, an ability to recognize the challenge, and a willingness to be a partner in adapting. Some misfits had humility and a desire to adapt, some didn't. Those who wanted to adapt, but were unable to do so, lacked grit. Those who didn't want to adapt were quicker to repurpose. Wondering what I mean?

Just as in the Rudolph story, the misfits aren't necessarily broken. They have just been in the wrong home. So—and this is often the case—rather than being misfits, some people are merely misplaced.

You are not the only one who will notice a misfit. Your team members will notice too. Depending on the culture of your team, they may or may not have shared this with you. In the culture I put in place, they share it freely with their managers. This feedback helps support transition into—or out of—the team.

If someone is a misfit, that person is not completely authentic with leaders. The only assumption I can make as to why they take this path is fear of losing their job. Authenticity must be achieved before trust can be established. But we're talking about misfits who will need to be removed from your team. How do you do this? There's a healthy way to do it, and then there's the way most managers do it.

We will start with the way most managers do it, because this is the one most will relate to. Have you ever had a personal relationship that had to end? How did it do so? When most people are young and just starting to form amorous relationships, these almost always end badly. They end with disagreements that leave both people angry and walking away. Ending a work relationship with a misfit can be much the same. I can think of several times when I had a work relationship end badly. One of the most memorable times was when a team member cursed me out, and when I turned my back to get paperwork for her, she threw her keys at my head like a 90-mile-an-hour fastball. She cursed and stomped her way out of the building. Not surprisingly, I was glad to be rid of her and never saw her again.

I was a highly respected leader and recognized for my high expectations for my team. She wasn't the only person who left in a rage. In fact, there was a time, many years ago, when that was the way most people left. At the time, I didn't think anything of it. Until one day, that is, when I was trying to recruit a really great candidate.

This woman was a top performer in the industry and a real catch. I tried to convince her to join my team. She sounded eager and said she would get back to me. A few days later I hadn't heard from her. I waited a couple more days, and still heard nothing, so I reached out to check in with her. She informed me that she had been visiting with people who used to work for me, and as much as she was flattered that I was trying to recruit her, she wasn't interested.

I did some digging to find out who she may have talked with. As it turns out, one of her friends was the woman who threw her keys at my head! I had not given that person another thought after she stormed out, but the reality is that her exit had a ripple effect on my personal brand. This was an epiphany for me. You see, at that point in my life, my work relationships were ending similar to how a personal relationship would end. I needed to reevaluate my approach. With that in mind, I began to construct a healthy way to part with misfits. That shift in my mind-set and behavior would become a positive part of my leadership legacy. I am going to share my approach and how I train leaders to partner with team members. For the purpose of this illustration, let's call the potential misfit Jack.

Jack's acclimation is being observed by you and your team. Jack's direct supervisor has been chosen to be his buddy and support his adaptation to the team. You determine that you should meet with Jack weekly to find out how he feels his transition is going. Be sure to share all positive feedback and observed behaviors with him. Ask Jack what challenges he is facing. Are his challenges consistent with what you have observed? If not, go deeper in your conversations with him and see if the challenges surface. If Jack is a misfit who might have to move on to another company, it is likely those challenges won't come out.

You need to share with him the challenges that have been observed. Brainstorm with him how to move through these and the positive intentions behind your plans to support his integration. Ask for his ideas and how he will hold himself accountable to the behavioral changes you've both brainstormed. End the meeting on a positive note, and clarify that he has your full support.

Observe him throughout the following week; check up on how Jack is doing. Share your observations with him. Hopefully, you are noticing positive behaviors you can acknowledge. Once again, ask him how he believes things are going. This conversation should sound similar to the one from the week before. If Jack has not followed through on the things he committed to, you will have to talk about those things and find out why he hasn't honored his commitment. In this scenario, the coaching will have a slightly heavier tone than the conversation you had earlier. Why? Because if Jack isn't honoring his commitments, your tone needs to echo the weight that lack of execution represents.

What obstacles have gotten in Jack's way? He is likely to mention just about anything but himself. (Remember, earlier, when we discussed humility and a desire to change.) If he does this, you must redirect him to what is within his control, which are his own behaviors. Once Jack recognizes that he is in control of his actions, get a new commitment from him. When you wrap up this latest conversation, let him know he has your support, and let Jack know you hope to celebrate his successes the next time you chat.

When you have your next meeting with Jack, if there has still been little to no progress, the conversation must be more serious. Hopefully, by that time, Jack comes forth with the true reasons he has not honored his commitment. If not, ask for clarity. Acknowledge that he did not honor his last two rounds of commitments. Ask him what he would do if he were in your shoes. Give him space—in a word, silence—to ponder this question and respond. Once he has answered, express your concerns that your company may not be the right fit for him. Share your observations from his original job interview with his present behavior. Seek to discover what changed regarding his enthusiasm.

If his answers reveal he has become disenchanted, let him know it's OK if the position isn't working for him, and that you want him to be happy. If he needs to move on, let him know you support him in his decision. Jack may say he wants to keep trying at your company, or he may be relieved that you are making it OK to leave. However it ends, you are in a good place with Jack.

If his choice was to stay and try to make it work, but is unable to do so for whatever reason, he will seek opportunities elsewhere without you having to suggest it again. When you meet with him again, he will likely give his notice. Regardless of the outcome, appreciate his partnership in the journey and wish him the best. In his initial interview, you saw something in Jack that moved you to offer him a role on your team. Though he was a misfit for your team, he will be a great fit in someone else's organization.

Once Jack has moved on, what will be his perception of you as a leader? What I've found is that by being a partner and transparent in all things, most people walk away with appreciation.

How does that reflect on your leadership legacy?

_____

_____

_____

_____

_____

The difference is as clear as night and day, especially when compared to my experiences from the past. If Jack were to receive a call from a friend asking about whether to consider a role with your team, the feedback is going to be very different. Only good things can come when you end a relationship in an honest and supportive way.

What about those initial misfits who do acclimate? These are your "Rudolphs." There will be team members who struggle in the beginning but will make the commitment and follow through and rise above the challenges. In time, their unique talents will elevate the entire team. Being different isn't bad, and if they can find a purpose for themselves within the team, they will add something you didn't have before.

Watching a potential misfit commit to change and then implementing the necessary changes is amazing. Sometimes I think it's the hope of landing a Rudolph that inspires leaders to hire some of the people who end up being misfits. They remember hiring such a person with similar attributes, and that person has since become a star among the group.

Who is someone you hired who turned out to be a Rudolph? What great attribute did they add to your team?

_____

_____

_____

_____

Hiring managers will take some risks in the selection process. If they didn't, you would never have a Rudolph and the magic that person can bring. How can you spot a Rudolph in the selection process? It isn't always easy. The key attribute to look for is self-accountability. When a person accepts full responsibility for their choices, both past and present, you may have a Rudolph. It is rare to find a candidate who immediately fits into your culture and team. If only it were that easy, right?

CHAPTER 8

"I'M SORRY YOU TOOK IT THAT WAY"

If we could elevate the words we use and the sentences we choose, we could elevate everything about our lives. Relationships would be impacted for the positive. Businesses and lives would change.

Words are currency.

Tammy Kling, CEO of OnFire Books (www.OnFireBooks.com) said those words in her TEDx talk, and they are true. What words can you inject into your culture and team to explain the way you really feel about defining your mission statement? Often people use words that are disempowering whether they realize it or not.

From time to time I've heard the phrase, "I'm sorry you took it that way!" Immediately, this gives me pause. This is clearly a passive-aggressive phrase. It's a negative phrase. It's a phrase that does not impact lives for the positive.

This phrase has so many communication errors. Have you ever said this, or something similar to it, to someone? Has it been said to you? What, exactly, is being apologized for? Let's break it down.

I'm sorry: The person speaking begins the statement of "apologizing" . . .

You: But the focus goes on the other person, not the person supposedly doing the apologizing.

Took it that way: . . . for the way the person *not* apologizing understood the information!

Do you see the irony in that? Backhanded, less-than-transparent communication serves no one. This is a phrase no leader should use—ever.

I grew up in a business world where this was a common phrase. In fact, I'm sure I have used it at one point or another, although I cringe thinking of it even now. I am sure there are businesses where this and several other terrible phrases are still used. While maturing as a leader, I began to realize that I was responsible for how someone took what I said, so learning a better way to communicate my message was necessary. You want to be sure that the intention of your words, and the way your words are received, are in alignment. In order to communicate in this way, you must have an understanding of how your audience communicates naturally.

> You want to be sure that the intention of your words, and the way your words are received, are in alignment.

When it comes to building teams and leaders, I find it extremely important to teach leaders how to communicate in a way that the audience receives the message the way it is intended. People speak in the way they are most comfortable being spoken to. This is usually effective with about one-fourth of your team. The learning comes from understanding how the other three-quarters of the team members speak and receive communication.

I have taught variations of DISC (designed by Dr. William Moulton; www.discprofile.com) and True Colors: Valuing

Differences (designed by Cindy Shaffer; www.truecolorsintl.com). Both models have similarities, and those who have experienced both can usually identify which quadrant from DISC is most like a color from True Colors.

When building healthy ways to communicate among diverse teams, I prefer True Colors: Valuing Differences. The way the different quadrants are named give no more strength to one over the other. What do I mean? With DISC, you have behavioral styles labeled as DRIVER, INFLUENTIAL, STEADY, and CONSCIENTIOUS. To me, this projects that DRIVER is the category you really want to be in if you work for a results-oriented company. Even though the categories are broken into even quadrants, the labels create stereotyping for those who took the class and reported back to me. I do not dislike the DISC program; it simply isn't the one I have found to be most effective in creating unity through understanding.

In True Colors, the model uses GOLD, ORANGE, BLUE, and GREEN to represent the different quadrants. There are two primary keys to communicating with another person. Are they more ask- or tell-assertive, or are they more task- or people-driven? These two determining differences make up the horizontal and vertical lines that create the quadrant. Working through the different behavior-style motivators of each color, as well as the major stressors for each, you help people discover their comfort in communicating. This is not a fast process, and over several hours together you begin to see understanding set in and shoulders relax.

Once a new team has grasped this, you can support conversations and conflicts in a healthy manner. As the team continues to work together, you find that conflicts through communication become few and far between. They also understand the absolute necessity to have a balance of all four colors to sustain a healthy team. Depending on the number of leaders for your environment, the same is true among the group. The more balance you have in styles, the more sustainable healthy communication will be.

Now, this doesn't mean that everyone walks away liking one another or becoming the best of friends. What you do have, though, is a common understanding of how to acclimate to your audience and yet remain authentic. Of course, you need to have hired people who value communication and trust and are humble enough to want and accept change.

Back to the opening statement: "I'm sorry you took it that way." The evolved team member is more likey to seek to understand what they said that made someone feel a certain way, and to find a way to fix it. They may clarify what their intention was, but they will always sincerely apologize for how they made the other person feel. They now have an understanding that you can't argue how someone else feels. It is *their reality.*

> They now have an understanding that you can't argue how someone else feels.

The other piece to acknowledge here is that the person whose feelings were hurt is sharing how they feel. The trust it takes to bring that forward needs to be appreciated. So many companies and teams lack the core values to support this sort of environment. Some companies almost encourage their people to keep their feelings to themselves.

The same can be true for relationships with a pattern of verbal abuse. If you've been taught that what you say won't be well received, you will naturally shut down. In corporations, leaders often bring their habits and actions with them from their childhood or previous jobs.

Whenever you hire new people who have worked for other companies, they invariably bring habits from those previous cultures. For those who come from an environment with broken communication, the new person nearly always lacks trust. How do you encourage someone who has been burned by another company to trust you? Well, it takes time and evidence that being forthright is viewed as a positive extension of trust by their new team. A great example of this comes to mind.

Many years ago, I hired a young lady named Sally to join our sales team. During our first meeting, she was confident and assertive. When you are hiring people who will interact with strangers and need to create a great experience, these are wonderful qualities to have. Through our conversations, I knew Sally was someone we wanted to join our team. The leadership team that would be responsible for her training and development also agreed.

When Sally started, however, it was obvious she struggled with trust. Not just in her teammates, but also with her leaders. Sally was always trying to figure out what the real purpose was behind someone's kind gestures. Noticing this, I sat with her to explore where this mind-set was coming from. During her extensive career with her previous company, she was able to assess that the kind gestures of others usually had an ulterior motive. The longer Sally worked there, the quicker she was able to pinpoint what those motives were. As years progressed, she had become comfortable enough to express concerns she would observe. But not only were these observations not met with appreciation, they created a sort of retaliatory response from her supervisors. The burn she felt from these circumstances carried through with her to her next company as habits. Sally knew what backlash felt like, and she had no intention of getting burned again.

Joining this new company, she committed to herself that she would go to work, do a great job, and go home. She wouldn't interact with others, where the potential outcome might be a social one, or establish a false sense of trust. She came into the new company with the intention of only depending on herself. As we sat and chatted about her transition, the only things she expressed were positive points about the team. When I asked if she had any questions for me, she said no.

You can't force someone to trust. The deeper the wound in this area, the longer it can take for it to occur. However, trust is at the very core of healthy communication, which in turn is at the heart of being able to grow your life (work, personal, or spiritual) in a significant way.

Time passed and Sally remained part of the team. Slowly, we began to see glimpses of trust from her to her team and leaders. We observed that, when she was sharing her concerns, her body language was, at first, tense. After a while she began to relax, and the more Sally was able to be authentic, without fear of retaliation, the more she flourished. Her words and actions were now aligned. She didn't work with fear of backlash for being genuine.

Sally's strength in knowledge, product, and now trust became a cornerstone others looked to—and strived for. Sally not only went on to be a healthy, productive member of the team, she created a personal brand around herself that resonated through the entire organization.

Though I have hired and observed thousands of new people, Sally remains one of the greatest transformation stories. Her work wounds had been so deep most would have believed it impossible for her to change. Supervisors had a belief that her healing—and becoming a healthy part of their team—was nearly impossible. However, we never gave up on her. It takes great strength to protect yourself like that, and we knew we could help her realize that not only was she safe, we would celebrate her brilliance. I was blessed to watch her celebrated at a recent banquet, and when the entire room stood to applaud, she was moved to joyful tears.

You may have heard it said that the most difficult customers can become the most loyal if you are able to earn their trust. The same is true when it comes to team members. Are you up for the challenge?

As you think about a team member(s) you might be challenged in communicating with, what might you do differently to foster healthy communication?

_____

_____

_____

_____

_____

In what way can you encourage and build trust within your personal relationships or home? Trust takes time, and it may not be about you at all. Someone who doesn't even know you can have preconceived notions or a history of experiences that damage the way they relate, communicate, and trust. We've all heard people relate horror stories from high school when a mean girl or someone they knew criticized or made fun of them. No one is immune to thoughtless comments by others.

If someone believed the negative comments of others or was betrayed early in life by a friend, trust can be a dominant issue in their life. Trust can be broken by colleagues, family members, and friends. Trust can be fractured by relationships or divorce. I mention all of these elements in business and life combined because your life and everyone else's is impacted by interactions with others. It may take a long time to build trust and communication with someone who has been burned.

I have been accused of trusting too quickly—and trusting again, even after being burned. What does that mean? There are people who have broken my trust and caused me great pain, yet I forgave them. How? I realize that others' choices are not my choices. Though they may impact me, was being malicious—toward me—their goal? Most times, it was not. The statement "We hurt those that are closest to us" comes to mind. If the act impacted me, it also impacted trust. Through conversation and seeking to understand the reasoning, we were able to work toward deep trust again. As I think of people I have been in the trenches with, there are some very important people I would have missed out on life with if I didn't believe the way I do.

What about those people I didn't move forward with in a relationship of trust? I found their choices to be ones I could not support. By maintaining a relationship with someone—amorous or friendship— you tether it to your being. That can be a hard pill to swallow. I get it. In 2010, I found myself in a sandpit of chaos when it came to personal relationships. I took pause while in the midst of that period and allowed myself the space to deeply reflect on each relationship, one by one. I had some connections that were just toxic, for myself and my values. Over the next couple of months, I ended several friendships. What I found on the other side of doing this was peace. I lovingly reflect on this year as 2010: The Year of the Purge.

> By maintaining a relationship with someone—amorous or friendship—you tether it to your being.

What are some of your core values on which you will not compromise?

_____

_____

_____

_____

_____

CHAPTER 9

MY FAVORITE "F" WORD

You read that chapter title correctly.

Where your mind went and what I mean are very different, though. My favorite "F" word is *filter*. How many times have you said something you wish you could take back? I call those times my "jelly donut" moments. My filter is off, and before I know it, the words are out there and cannot be taken back. Nearly every time I do this I feel remorse. Remorse for the person who was on the receiving end, and remorse for my lack of self-control.

As Tammy Kling expresses, *Words Are Currency*™, the reverse of that can also be true. Words can be a debt. If you value the person you were talking to you, will try to regain ground in your relationship with them. Your unfiltered words caused your relationship account to make an unauthorized debit.

How do you filter your thoughts? A lot depends on you and the filters you choose to value. The more you create the habit of filtering your words before speaking, the easier it will become. Engaging your filter doesn't mean you're selling yourself out. It simply means you're being a leader. Leaders engage their mind before their mouth. Leaders provide thoughtful consideration to a topic before they talk to or shout at or condemn another human. Even if it's not about someone else, and even if you're absolutely correct, a leader realizes there are times when your opinion should remain just that: your opinion. A leader isn't driven by the desire to be right. A leader is driven by the desire to make everything and everyone better and to get the team aligned and focused on the right goals.

Of course, we've all made mistakes!

Need some examples? Here are three basic questions used by many:

- Is it truthful?

- Is it kind?

- Is it necessary?

And, of course, there are times when being silent is the best course of action.

When you are thoughtful about your words, what are the filters you put your thoughts through before they come out as words?

_____

_____

_____

_____

_____

Here's another filter you can use. Anytime you are about to start a sentence with "I don't mean to be disrespectful" or, "With all due respect," make the decision to rethink your thoughts into something more productive. Any sentence that begins in such a way is never positive. *These statements convey that the very thing mentioned is about to occur with your words. "I don't mean to be disrespectful" translates to "I am about to be quite disrespectful."*

I imagine your wheels are turning. You're wondering why, on one hand, I say you should be authentic, and on the other hand I am telling you to filter your thoughts. How do these go together?

> Being authentic means being aligned with who you are as a person and being bold enough to be you.

Being authentic means being aligned with who you are as a person and being bold enough to be you. Being authentic does not mean you should create a verbal bulldozer and run other people over. You cannot do that and try to justify it by saying you were being authentic. Leaders find a way to be authentically truthful. It's possible.

The filter that has served me the most has been humility.

When I was younger, being humble and being bold seemed nearly contradictory. So I chose bold almost every time. It wasn't until I was in my thirties that I found the beautiful relationship between the two. Actions are important to me, and I have always been results focused. As a leader, I have made it a point to exceed every goal I possibly could. Though there would be a miss here and there, I was able to bounce back quickly and continue to achieve. The day came in which I took on my pinnacle work goal. Pride was pouring from my soul. I couldn't wait to find out how elated the executives would be. What came next was far from elation.

I sat down to hear all the wonderful feedback about what an incredible leader I was, but what they shared was that they questioned whether I had the skill set to lead an elite-performing team. *Whoa! How dare they?* I developed that team, and I led that team to great success. Of course I had the skill!

I reeled about this for days. I wasn't sleeping, and I could tell people were all but avoiding me. Mentally, I bottomed out. That is where I found the filter of humility.

I stepped out of my body, looked at myself objectively, and applied the filter. If world-class executives were questioning my skill, then I had earned their concern. From this humble space, I reached out and thanked them for their candor. I also asked to be guided to what they believed I needed to confidently lead the elite group.

The skill I gained and the confidence I earned would have passed me by had I not filtered myself through humility. Today I teach this concept to everyone I choose to work with and who chooses to work with me.

Think on this today: how can you exercise your personal filters and think cautiously about your feedback and words?

_____

_____

_____

_____

_____

CHAPTER 10

KEEP IT SHORT!

What's the best way to convey an idea? Whether it's a new concept, a training or sales program, or something to teach your kids, the very best way is to keep the person's attention. And keeping that person's attention is critical for success and learning, so the best way to do that is to keep it short.

While I was visiting family in Virginia, their neighbors, Kevin and Karen, were sharing their adopted puppy with all of us. Kevin was talking about training. He had trained several German Shepherds in the past, and he had found that the most effective training was to try some training exercises for five minutes in the morning and five minutes in the evening. After that amount of time, he said, the puppy gets frustrated, and so does the owner. As he shared this, I grabbed my phone to make a note, because this correlated to what I have trained leaders to do for years. Keep it short, and learning will occur much faster.

When I train leaders, I am very clear that fifteen minutes is the maximum amount of time that should be spent on such teaching.

When you exceed fifteen minutes, content begins to get lost, and the mind will digress. Rather than planning to sit with someone and teach an entire topic, break it down to what you can absolutely teach in fifteen minutes. With deliberate, focused training, the person being trained can closely focus on the content and walk away having learned something. Small progressive steps lead to positive momentum. Spend a few minutes to think on this. If you currently train others and plan an hour or, even worse, an entire day on training, how do you know what people are walking away with? Is the content sticking with them?

As a trainer, the side benefit of focusing on fifteen minutes is that you are extremely deliberate in your training plan.

Example: If you are in the mortgage business and you want to train someone on the laws surrounding your trade, there is no way you can teach them all and expect the information to be retained in one training session. When you look at the broad topic and challenge yourself to focus on learning that can happen in fifteen-minute segments, you will find it comes down to one to two takeaways that need to be remembered. Whether you are a trainer, coach, or parent, you will find yourself in a position to teach another.

With those you are charged to instruct, what is the topic you wish to teach? Feel free to jot these down below. If you have more than one topic, because maybe you're a parent, a supervisor, or coach, I will give you a bit more space to be sure you are able to list them all.

_____

_____

_____

_____

_____

_____

_____

_____

_____

_____

_____

OK. You have the topic outlined. As a parent, your topic may have been how to be a responsible adult. We will use that for the purpose of illustration. When you look at the phrase "Be a responsible adult," there is no way you can teach all this encompasses at one time. Agree? So, let's look at some ways you may break it down to learnable segments of time. Here are a few points I can think of that could be included:

1) Importance of punctuality

2) Relevance of verbal salutations

3) Honoring commitments

4) How to balance a checking account

5) Credit and how it works

Teaching a young person how to be a responsible adult can go on and on. As you look at the examples I shared, can these blocks be taught in fifteen-minute segments? Some can, but most will need repeating as well as dissection into smaller topics. As you look at the topics you listed above, break them down into subtopics here.

_____

_____

_____

_____

_____

_____

_____

_____

Here is where the traction comes in. As you look at your sub-topics, do you see that when all of the lessons are learned, they translate into the big topic being realized? If not completely, you should at least be able to see the framework in place. How can you be sure that learning occurred from the fifteen minutes you spent together? You should always get a commitment from the student to change what is observable. "Observable" means it is action you can see or results that can be measured. An example of this might be that the student commits to responding to elders with "No, sir," and "Yes, sir." As you watch them interact with someone older than themselves, you can see this occur. (Or not.)

Now review your subtopics. What might be some observable behaviors your student could commit to?

_____

_____

_____

_____

_____

Now, the idea isn't to have you ask them to commit to XYZ. Ideally, when the training is over and you ask what they have learned and how might you observe it in action, each should have their own specific ideas to share. The beauty in this is that when it is their idea, they are more likely to be committed to implementing it. As the teacher, when you see the action in motion, recognize it and celebrate the deliberate change. People tend to emulate what they are acknowledged for. Also, deliberate change in action begins to rewire a person's habit system. Before long, the change they were conscious of implementing becomes an unconscious habit. Your teaching has taken root. Appreciate this and continue the process.

> People tend to emulate what they are acknowledged for.

Even if you're not responsible to train others, you are absolutely responsible for your own development. The same concept applies. What is something you have really wanted to learn, but, for any reason, have not taken on the task of doing so?

As you consider this knowledge-based goal, is it something in which true learning can occur in fifteen minutes? Let's say you picked a task like cooking. You really want to learn to cook, but just haven't tackled it. Cooking is a big topic and too broad to learn in one training session. As we did before, let's break it down to smaller possible areas to take on for growth:

- How to scramble eggs and cook bacon
- How to make pancakes and waffles
- How to make spaghetti

The ability to master one of these entrees will help you learn more. Prep time to make any of the above dishes is less than fifteen minutes. What follows from there is execution. Practicing what you want to learn isn't inclusive to the time of *learning it*. You may be in the kitchen for thirty minutes to begin. In time, the more you learn to cook, the meals you learn to cook will become more complicated. With the knowledge gained from simpler skills, creating more complicated dishes will become simpler. If you entered into your cooking journey desiring to learn how to make chicken curry, but you didn't know how to cook the most basic recipes, the learning and prep time would not only be more than fifteen minutes, you would likely become frustrated and quit.

Tackling big tasks before learning the fundamentals can be intimidating at best and cause many to simply give up altogether. As humans, we don't like the feeling of failure. On a professional level, you are forced to move through your inexperience in order to effectively do your job. In your personal life, however, it is most likely that no one is going to force you to learn what you don't know. Using cooking as the example for personal growth, those of you who do not attempt this skill are probably thinking that you haven't learned it because you simply don't like to cook.

If that is truly the case, and not that you have tried to cook and failed, then bravo. Being true to who you are is commendable. However, in many cases, it is because the attempt was made, it failed, and you justify not trying again by saying you don't like to do it. Well, of course you didn't like it. Who likes to fail? Following this thought process, let's revisit the skill that you have really wanted to learn but have not yet done successfully.

Being true to yourself, what are the real reason(s) you haven't done so yet?

_____

_____

_____

_____

_____

As you review these reasons, mark the ones that are excuse based and thus cause you to not learn what you have wanted to learn. Things like "I don't have the time" would qualify to be marked out. When you're done, look at what remains. How might you move beyond the reason(s) and push yourself to grow in the area you really want to grow in?

Now, there is a chance that what you listed wasn't really true to your desires. If that's the case, you have no clarity at this moment on how to begin. So, go back to what you truly want to learn and think of something else. Repeat the steps that follow.

At this point you should have identified a task you want to learn, understand the excuses you have used that have stopped you, and then clarified how you will move past those excuses to begin. When to begin? As you consider what you want, it's time to make a commitment to starting the journey.

As you look at the topic, how will you move past the obstacles and when will you begin? How you will commit in a way that you cannot fail to start?

Here is where you should appreciate yourself. Appreciate that you have moved beyond excuses and that you're going to learn something you've been wanting to learn. You are not being forced to learn it for your occupation or to support others, but simply because it is important to you. Celebrate this! When you honor your commitment to yourself, it is just as important as honoring those commitments you make to others! Be true to your word

When you honor your commitment to yourself, it is just as important as honoring those commitments you make to others!

with yourself also. When you learn what it is you want to learn, there will be growth. From your growth, you become a better version of yourself, which supports those around you whom you love. Remember, for learning to occur, it must come in small brackets of time that make it effective.

Here's a tidbit you may be able to relate to. My son, Jordan, always said he didn't like to cook. From the time he was about twelve, I tried to get him in the kitchen as often as possible. Though he seemed to enjoy the time spent making a meal, he wouldn't attempt to cook on his own. As he grew older and began to want to prepare meals for others, he realized he wasn't comfortable cooking.

That was why he wasn't doing it. We went through the process of learning the very way I have walked through it in this chapter. As Jordan began to master breakfast (which are the simplest meals to learn, in my opinion), he moved on to other dishes. Today, Jordan makes a mean chicken curry, and he does it without recipes. He didn't start there, but he got to that place through his continued practice.

Practice, execute, and repeat. This is how you adopt what you learn into your habits. One day you will look back at where you started the journey and wonder what took you so long to begin. When that day comes, reach out and share with me how you did.

RELATIONSHIPS

WORK TOWARD A MASTER'S DEGREE

If I were to tell you that we are now going to discuss education, you might think I am speaking of an academic form of learning. However, this chapter is not about that.

It doesn't matter what you do or what your level of education is because you can always do and have and be more than you are today. This chapter is about receiving a master's degree in relationships. A master's in relationships is 100 percent up to you. It won't take you three or five years to obtain and hopefully won't cost you nearly as much money as an academic master's. A master's degree in relationships will transform and multiply your life and revenue far more than any degree on paper.

Be Intentional Today

The ultimate earning opportunity you can create is in making lifelong connections. And this requires intentionality. Who will you talk to today? What is your ultimate message and desired outcome? What will you say the moment you meet someone new?

Every time you meet someone new, whether socially or professionally, your journey toward a potential master's degree begins. The master's you have already earned in other relationships does not change, but for this new relationship the journey has just begun. Imagine that the other person doesn't know anything about you or how to handle conflict or the gifts you have inside. Strong and solid relationships begin with communication. This means listening as well.

Everything we explore together in this chapter can benefit you both personally and professionally, but here we are going to focus on work relationships. Why? Because you have complete control over who you have a connection with outside of the office, but let's face it: unless you are the hiring manager or sole decision-maker in your company, You will be forced to meet new people frequently. Some you'll have natural chemistry with, but there will be others who rub you the wrong way or take offense to your very presence for no reason at all. That's OK! We live on this planet with everyone else and you don't have to love every single individual you meet. But you will have to develop a relationship if you work with them. You won't be able to ignore them, talk down to them, or roll your eyes if you don't like them.

It is with these people that you will want to work toward a master's degree in relationships.

It has been said that all relationships start with a hello. I disagree. I believe they begin with an understanding of your gateways. When you meet someone new, what gate in your mind must open to enable you to be interested in getting to know that person better?

Imagine you are standing in front of a beautiful courtyard garden. You notice the beautiful flowers planted in a way that they soften the strength of the tall manicured shrubs that form walls around the courtyard. From where you are standing, you see that in order to walk through the garden you must pass through a series of gates. Each gate requires a key. Now, you can't open gate three until gate one opens because you can't even get to the third gate until you have passed through the first two.

What are the gates for you—those values that must be honored?

_____

_____

_____

_____

Are you with me? Using this analogy, I will share what it takes for someone to open the gates in my own courtyard of relationships. Yours may be different, and that is OK.

The first gateway is authenticity. Every person I meet is a unique composite of their own personal journey, but one thing they must be in order to pass through my gate is transparent. It is OK to be nervous. It is OK to be uncomfortable. When I am authentic toward the other person, it shows them that it is safe for them to be authentic in return.

You may be wondering: How do I know if a new person is being authentic when I don't even know them yet? That is a great question. In my experience I have noticed some common behaviors that throw up red flags when it comes to someone being genuine. Here are some examples of an individual's behavior that can prove to be red flags to the gateway of authenticity:

Over-complimentary toward others. Whenever someone approaches this type of person, they are showered with compliments on everything from their attire to the choices they have made or any number of other things.

Projecting negative comments to a third party. Within a short period of being on the team, they will approach teammates with comments or concerns about another team member. If they were truly looking for guidance, they would only approach the team member they are concerned about. When several team members are approached on the topic, that is when the red flag goes up. If you have the right culture, your team will act quickly and take those concerns to the appropriate people and they will be resolved. That is what a tribe of people with the same values do.

Their words and actions are not in alignment. If they say they are a positive person but all you see them do is pout and complain, there is a misalignment for certain. That almost certainly indicates a lack of authenticity.

With the first gate identified—hopefully, the new teammate embodies the value of authenticity—we are on to the second gateway.

The next gate represents humility, or the ability to be humble. You will read about this one more than once throughout this journey. In working toward a master's degree with a new teammate, it is important to observe this trait. We have already mentioned how working for a new company means having to learn new skills, and errors will occur. The ability to be humble is necessary for a new team member to grow past mistakes. Humility couples well with authenticity, but the presence of one does not necessarily mean the presence of the other.

I have known great people who were humble, yet I never got to see who they really were because being authentic was a challenge for them. I have also known people who were truly authentic, yet they wouldn't admit to an error unless they were caught actually making it. If you think about all the people you have known, I am sure you can remember people like that. Hopefully, you will also remember people who lived a humble and authentic life.

It is important to be aware of those people who outwardly behave as if they are humble, but their actions prove otherwise.

Here is a key difference: A person who is humble will do something for someone—without expecting something in return.

For example, a teammate asks to switch scheduled shifts with someone. They make the switch. The person who agreed to the switch, merely pretending to be humble, will likely tell everyone on the team how selfless they were in helping the other person out. They might even find a way to drop a hint to a supervisor about what a great teammate they are because they made such a sacrifice.

Does that example bring to mind anyone you know? It does not mean they have ill intentions, but they are not being genuinely humble. One of the most consistent behaviors I have observed from people lacking humility is a general lack of ownership for errors. When someone tries to share with them something that was done incorrectly, they become immediately defensive and try to justify why it was done that way. Entering a new company comes with a learning curve, and errors are expected. A humble team member will not only own up to errors, he or she will seek help on how to do it better next time.

How can you tell if someone is humble? There are several behaviors that are representative; here are a few of the more common behaviors I have noticed.

They don't talk about themselves unless they have been asked. What do I mean? A humble teammate asks how you are doing because they really want to know. They speak from a place of gratitude and appreciation nearly all the time. Their energy and their example encourages you to be a better person.

They notice what people don't say, and act accordingly. I think one of the best examples of humility is when one provides food for another. Have you ever noticed a fellow teammate who did not eat when it was their lunch break? Not because they were busy, but because they did not have anything to eat? I have seen this, and I have seen a fellow teammate frequently step up and share their food. After a while, that same teammate began bringing extra food every day to share with the person who had nothing. How often do you think that person let everyone know how great they were by sharing their food? That's right: never.

As you consider authenticity and humility, who are the people in your life that come to mind as the very best examples of these two values?

_____

_____

_____

_____

_____

The third gateway, perhaps the most important one to me, is trust. Why is this the last one? In the workplace, trust should be earned. Period.

Trust means you believe someone is being honest, making the best decisions they can, and want only what is best for the team. If trust is given out too quickly, you risk damaging relationships in which you have already earned a master's degree. How? You may side with a new team member in a situation they have manipulated to earn favor.

Believe me, it happens. When people join a new company, they bring with them habits from previous work environments. While some of these habits are healthy, you will find there are some that are toxic. The only way to ensure you don't allow these toxic habits to erode your culture is to guard against them until the intention of the person is truly understood.

Please note that it is OK to let a new team member know what your gateways are. If you are a transparent person and you can see the other person is struggling with how to connect with you, share it with them. What I have found over the last twenty-plus years is that sincere communication is missing in most work environments. When candor comes from a place of care, it is appreciated, understood, and—if the person is up to working toward a master's—accepted.

I can recall a time when a new team member was struggling to open the gates to a master's. This person was struggling with nearly everyone, but they seemed especially concerned about getting there with me. In a conversation, a teammate expressed that she hoped she hadn't lost my trust.

I told her she hadn't lost my trust because she had not earned it yet. Her expression told me she was puzzled, so I walked her through the journey for us to earn a master's degree. I also shared with her what gate she was at at that point in our relationship. As a leader, it is my duty to protect the ability of the team to earn the monies needed to support their families. But when someone manages to earn a master's with me, it transcends our relationship in the workplace. Today, I have people I mentor from twenty years ago, and I still feel a responsibility to support them in any way I can.

You might think that letting the person know they had not yet earned my trust was upsetting for them, but the effect was quite the opposite. When you live the values you expect of another person, your intentions become obvious through your behavior. Her appreciation was obvious, and her behaviors afterward seemed a bit more relaxed. She began working toward her master's degree with me.

> When you live the values you expect of another person, your intentions become obvious through your behavior.

Once all three gates have been opened, that team member has a lifelong place in my garden. If you are a leader, your responsibility to your team goes beyond the company within which you forged your relationships. If you are in leadership because you want to support others and you want to ensure success for those who trust you to lead them, then you understand this way of thinking. Even if you do not have an official title, when you have gotten your master's degree in relationships, you have likely had teammates want to follow you when you switched companies. This is because once you earn your master's degree, it is a relationship that will not be defined by one particular company.

List people you have gotten to a master's degree in relationship with. How have these relationships proven a positive impact in your life?

_____

_____

_____

_____

_____

How long should it take to reach this kind of relationship with someone? The most truthful answer is: as long it takes. You may work with people for years and not achieve a master's. Others may join your team, and it is forged quickly. Whether or not a master's is achieved doesn't mean you can't have a positive working relationship. Should either of you let go of your position and move to another company, it is unlikely you will stay in touch, and that is completely normal. Sometimes people come into our lives for a season, and then the season passes. However you earn your master's degree, appreciate the journey.

Revisit the values you mentioned near the beginning of this chapter. Has the order shifted at all? Take a moment to list, in order, your gateways. Changed or not, this is an area that is important for you to know—and honor—for yourself.

_____

_____

_____

_____

_____

_____

_____

CHAPTER 12

CAN YOU REPEAT THAT, PLEASE?

What happens to the person on the other end of the phone line or conversation when you don't listen? How do they *really* feel or think about observing you not listening, even though they pretend not to notice?

We have all been guilty of this.

Someone is talking to us, and then they ask a question—and you have to ask them to repeat the question. Or, someone is talking, and before they have even finished what they are saying, we inter-ject—or *interrupt* would be a better way of describing the action. As you think about these two scenarios, can you recall a time you have done one or both of these actions?

What about the flip side of this situation? You are speaking, yet you feel as if the other person isn't listening to what you said—at all. Have you ever had to repeat the question? How about being inter-rupted mid-speech? Listening truly is an art.

How does it make you feel when someone disregards your words? What I have found is

> Listening truly is an art.

that it makes the person who was speaking feel as though what they are saying isn't important. In building relationships, how do you believe this plays into that dynamic? No one wants to talk to someone who treats them with disrespect.

For better understanding, let's call the person speaking "The Voice," and the person who interrupts, or simply isn't listening, "The Squirrel."

The Squirrel's mind is in one hundred different places when The Voice walks up and wants to have a conversation. The Squirrel acknowledges The Voice, and The Voice launches into what he wants to talk about. The Squirrel is listening, in the beginning, and then she finds her mind wandering. She begins to think about what she needs to accomplish for the day.

Her thoughts go back to what she was doing earlier that morning. The Squirrel's mind may even go to a moment far in the future. As The Squirrel's mind is deep into her own thoughts, she can "hear" The Voice talking, but she isn't truly listening. The Voice asks a question, and The Squirrel doesn't answer, even though she is clearly still physically present. The Voice addresses The Squirrel again. Oops! The Squirrel quickly comes back to the moment, apologizes that she didn't hear the question, and asks The Voice to repeat it . . .

I also mentioned The Interrupter earlier. So, let's visit The Voice and The Squirrel on a different day. The Voice approaches The Squirrel to talk about the upcoming changes in the office. As The Voice speaks, The Squirrel is completely aware of what The Voice is saying, and it brings up deep thoughts inside The Squirrel. The Squirrel's thoughts are so top of mind, so to speak, that she is waiting for The Voice to take a breath so she can share her incredible thoughts around this topic. The Squirrel waits—and, in her mind—waits. There it is! The Voice is taking a breath! The Squirrel begins to speak, but The Voice wasn't really finished with his thoughts. With what The Squirrel found to be an opportunity to speak, she was clearly speaking over The Voice. The Squirrel apologizes for interrupting.

As you reflect on these scenarios with The Voice and The Squirrel, think about a time you have been The Voice. How did you feel during those chats?

_____

_____

_____

_____

_____

Now, think about a time you have been The Squirrel. How did you feel during those chats?

_____

_____

_____

_____

Are you asking yourself why we are talking about this now? When it comes to relationships and rapport, not truly listening can be a major roadblock—and you may not even be aware of it. To truly listen to another, you must be fully present. Fully present? Your *mind* has to be there along with your body. In the first scenario, this is easy to acknowledge. In the second scenario, you may think The Squirrel was fully present, but she wasn't. You see, when her mind was wrapped around what her response would be to what The Voice was saying, she couldn't truly listen to what was being said to her. The Squirrel's mind had gone to what her own words would be and, therefore, she wasn't fully present in the conversation as it was happening.

So which one are you?

The side effect of not truly listening—not being fully present in a conversation—impacts how others see us. It also impacts how they perceive we feel about them. Look at your answers, above, when it came to how you felt. As you consider your feelings, then, would you want others to feel that way when they walk away from a conversation with you?

I have found two primary reasons conversations like these happen. When The Voice had to repeat the question, The Squirrel's mind was simply elsewhere when The Voice approached and began speaking. In the second scenario, when The Squirrel jumped in with her thoughts, mid-speech of The Voice, she was struggling to control her thoughts and, as many will say, she "didn't want to forget" what she had in mind to share.

OK, here's the good news. With awareness comes the opportunity to change things. Now, if you've read this chapter thus far and believe you a truly great listener—and you are never The Squirrel—bravo! Truly. In my career, I have come across a few of you who truly understand this—and exercise it—consistently. For the other 99.9 percent of us, I want to encourage us that there is hope. How we listen isn't a born trait. Since it isn't preconstructed in our DNA, that means it is a habit we create. Habits can be changed; we just have to choose to notice the problem and then work to make the change.

> How we listen isn't a born trait.

If someone approaches to engage in a conversation, and you are mentally knee-deep in a task, planning, or the like, it's OK to express that to other person. You may say something like, "Voice, I really want to hear what you are saying, and at the moment, my mind is tightly wrapped around this task. Would it be OK if I finish this, and then we chat? I want to give you my full attention, and I don't think I can in this very moment." Though The Voice may look disappointed at not being able to launch into his dialogue, he will understand and appreciate the care you showed. Now, once you are free in your mind, it is equally important that you circle back to The Voice and encourage him to share what he wanted to talk about earlier. Sometimes, he will still want to chat. Other times, he will say it wasn't important, or he has already worked it out, something along those lines. In either scenario, your relationship didn't take a communication hit.

OK: Operation Interruptus. This one can be a bit trickier in rewiring your habit. If you're someone whose mind is constantly running at 100 miles per hour, you most likely find this person to be you—and often. Those around you have chalked it up to that's "just who you are." As comfortable as that may seem, it is still a roadblock to strong relationships—and one I hope you want to change. How do you fully listen and, when a thought comes up, not jump in? It can be different for every person, but I will share some best practices with you. The first part, though, is to determine your habit and why you interrupt.

"I don't want to forget my thought. " If this is your primary Interruptus excuse, the reality is that if the person quits speaking and your thought is gone, was it really that important to the conversation? Did its absence find the whole of the conversation lacking traction because you didn't immediately share what was on your mind? I'm going to go with no on that one! The truth is by not interjecting for the reason that you didn't want to lose your thought, you allowed the flow of the conversation to continue.

If others are present and listening (such as during a training session or a meeting), your discipline in not interrupting allowed everyone else to stay on course with the thoughts of the speaker. Though you may have a moment of sadness that you didn't jump in and share that bright thought, appreciate the control you showed in not disrupting the content.

How do you begin to do this? If you are in a training/meeting, jot a quick note—a word that will trigger that thought again should you find it impactful to share—but only once the person speaking is finished. To fully give your mind back to the speaker, focus on the message they are currently delivering. By focusing on message words (those words that call to action in the presentation), your mind can reconnect with the speaker—and move beyond your own thoughts.

What about when you are in a one-on-one conversation? Jotting a word down and breaking eye contact shouldn't be done. Instead, focus on the impact word(s) the other person is saying in real time, and allow yourself to reconnect to the conversation. If you forget what you were going to say, it is OK! The positive impact of your being fully present and listening is far more relevant than the fleeting thought you never shared. Appreciate your control. Appreciate your presence.

LISTEN TO HEAR. DO NOT LISTEN TO SPEAK.
(This is a favorite quote I share with people when I am teaching them to actively listen.)

Here's a great nugget to understand how these actions impact your habits. The more often you change how you listen in a conversation—truly listen—the more it becomes your new habit. In time, you will find you won't have to be so deliberate to make different choices in the moment to be fully present—the actions will come naturally. You will be *you*—and with it, a great listener who is respected by others.

Listening could be the greatest secret weapon you deploy from your toolbox in the business world. So few people listen. If you do, you'll be the one to stand out.

CHAPTER 13

THE LENSES ARE FREE

The funny thing about something being free is that things that are not purchased or earned are typically neglected. Have you ever noticed that? I can recall my mom making various comments in this regard throughout my childhood. "Do you know how much that costs?" she would ask. "You're just tossing it around as though it has no value. One day, you will be the one paying for such things, and then you will understand."

I believed her, of course, but the truth of her words did not sink in until the time came when I was the one buying—and watching things be treated with little to no value. There are more important things in life that we can take for granted. We could go down a rabbit hole on this one, but I want to focus on one thing. If you choose to value this one thing, it can change your life:

> You hold the lenses of choice.

You hold the lenses of choice.

"Lenses" are the way you look at situations, information, and circumstances. The way in which you process life is interesting. You build assumptions based on similar situations and their outcomes from your past. Those assumptions helped create your own customized lenses through which you view life. How you see, feel, and express your reactions flows from your view of things. You may not realize it, but those closest to you can probably predict how you are going to view a situation and respond. What if I told you that you can change your lenses? You can decide to reprogram how your lenses show you situations, information, and circumstance. I wouldn't have believed it if I hadn't managed to do so myself many years ago.

There had been plenty of times in my life that others didn't agree with me or my viewpoint. I chalked it up to them not seeing the full picture or, even worse, being inferior in their ability to process information and come to the correct answer. One day, I was driving to work and chatting on the phone with Greg Johnson, the founder of Night of Superstars, a children's charity I had recently become involved with. He was speaking when I noticed a traffic jam up ahead.

I chimed out something like, "Oh, great. Of course traffic is going to be stopped!"

Greg said, "Think about the blessing that you are stuck in traffic, and not the reason traffic isn't moving."

The calm in his statement and the loving intention of it stunned me into silence. I had not considered that, and he was right. He could hear my affirmation in the silence, and he shared with me that to be joyful is a choice. The children we support in Night of Superstars have incredible adversities they didn't ask for, and they don't complain about what they have been dealt. They rise above it. They are so inspirational, and when we celebrate them and their achievements, they radiate joy.

People attend the event believing it is going to be sad, but after being exposed to the joy of the children, they walk away completely uplifted and in awe.

When I finally made it to work, my conversation with Greg continued to resonate inside of me. Could I look at situations the way Greg and the young superstars did? I began to challenge myself to pause and ask myself how the lenses of joy would view a particular situation. What if I adopted a lens of joy? It took conscious effort not to react out of habit and allow myself a few extra moments to process. It was such a different lens for me that sometimes I struggled to decipher the view. As days turned into months, I found that I didn't have to be so deliberate anymore. I had managed to reset my lenses, and through that I began to help others do the same.

If you had to choose a primary filter for your lenses, what would that be and why?

_____

_____

_____

_____

_____

With joy being the definition of my lenses, I found other values show up that sharpened my view. Positive intention, humility, and grace started to integrate. But how?

Positive intention came first. This lens supports the belief that everything has a positive intention. Whether it is the choices and action of others, hitting every red light downtown, or even a disappointment at work, there is positive intention. When you believe this to be so and begin to apply this to your lenses, everything transforms and beauty appears. Positive intention is an ingredient that supports joy. It is easier to feel joyful when you are guided by a positive intention. By contrast, when I picked apart a circumstance and analyzed how I was slighted, I never felt happy on the other side.

In reevaluating such times through the lens of positive intentions, I could appreciate the gift that I received. From hard experiences came patience, learning, and the opportunity to execute even better. No one wants to think of those things when disappointment strikes, but if you can make yourself do so and seek the positive intention, the blow is certainly lessened.

Humility followed. For me, it almost seemed as though it came in to my lenses through the shadows. When I looked for the positive intention for me, it wasn't always there. When I looked closer, I could see where the positive intention was for another person, and I appreciated that too. I wasn't elated, but the appreciation I felt for the other person began to bring more joy than if it had been my own. To be able to see how the situation would support someone I cared about helped steer me away from my past habit (lens) of feeling sorry for myself. Supporting others is at the core of my joy.

Grace appeared. The gift given, but not deserved, had moved into my lenses. This was an interesting acclimation, because it found me thanking God out loud—and often. I have always felt a close connection, but it was reserved for morning and evening conversations between the two of us. Now, my sense of appreciation was not scheduled, and it happened throughout my days. It wasn't that I fell to my knees and began to pray, but I would look up, acknowledge Him in the event, and give my thanks. My relationship had become even stronger because the lens I was seeing through brought clarity. With grace present, I was able to forgive faster and easier.

Another shift that happened with my lens upgrade was the ability to recognize what defines the lenses of others. Now, to be clear, understanding doesn't mean judging. Having an understanding, though, has helped me to support others with redefining the lenses they use. When you want the best for others, this is a no-brainer.

Does all of this apply to work? Absolutely. Every day, depending on how many people you interact with, there are dozens of moments when people are viewing life through their own particular lenses. When people come to me griping about what someone else has done, I ask them to look through the other person's lenses. Why might they have chosen to do what they did? Do they truly believe the other person is bad and motivated by malicious intent? The conversation that follows usually results in the complainer becoming calm. If a person does not calm down, I sometimes have to be firm with them. Sometimes you have to put a stick in the spokes to motivate a shift in the lenses. With enough effort, you can usually get the person to come around. If someone has chosen you to be the one they complain to, it is up to you to help shift their perspective. If you just let them vent or look for your input with no redirection, you are not only breaking the process to help them shift, you are taking on poison that will likely taint your own lenses.

We all have lenses we use to justify the ending we project. The best example of this is when someone is generally unhappy and seeking change. Most often, we don't look inside ourselves to find the unrest and resolve it. We look externally, and we begin to want change. Let's say you express something like, "If I were happier at home, I would be happier at work." By doing that you focus your attention on your home life, and you begin to pick apart every situation that upsets you. The result is that you become even more upset. If you have directed your unhappiness toward a spouse or partner, you can begin to not even like them anymore. What you used to find cute in the one you love becomes a source of anger and frustration.

When it comes to work, you see the hot spots in your day. You become increasingly frustrated, and when you apply your lenses, you feel justified for feeling as you do. You stop appreciating the positives and your teammates, and you isolate yourself from others. Unless someone points it out to you, you don't even notice. The lenses of justification are terribly toxic.

When the lenses we use are negative, the outcome is the same.

What started as a journey to be happy again results in terrible outcomes. You may find happiness for a short while, but when unhappiness visits again, the cycle will begin anew.

Imagine when you are unhappy that you can look inside and find out why. You choose lenses of retrospect, and you began to unravel what led you to be unhappy. From this viewpoint, you make shifts in your actions that make you feel happy again. When everything inside you is aligned, your lenses are in focus. Appreciation shows up and life is good. This isn't to say that all change in life is unnecessary, but a lot of changes that occur when we are not using the right lenses is a loss. Have you ever left a relationship and, looking back, wish you would have tried harder? What about a job?

Jumping from job to job or relationship to relationship doesn't help you grow as a human being. I spent my twenties doing this, seeking happiness when it was gone and jumping ship with relationships and work. The real magic didn't begin to happen until I looked inside myself and began to define the lenses I wanted to use.

I began this part of our journey with how we take for granted what is free. The lenses are out there to use. They are free for you to choose, regardless of which ones you choose. Even though they are free, can you value the ones you have? Do they support your outcome, or do they bring clarity to what is around you? Is the outcome positive, or do you find yourself full of negative thoughts and words? Whether you choose lenses that are positive or negative, your investment is the same.

How might you choose to see situations through the lenses of a positive outcome?

_____

_____

_____

_____

_____

CHAPTER 14

RELATIONSHIPS RULE!

Think about your life and the relationships that matter most to you. Outside of family, how many people come to mind that you believe you have a strong relationship with?

Jot down the names that come to mind. Keep writing until you run out of names or run out of lines to write on.

_____

_____

_____

_____

_____

Look at the list of names. Why did you think of them? At the core of the word *relationship* is the root word *relate*. How do you relate to those special people in your life? With family, for example, though challenges occur, you usually navigate through them with a sense of unconditional love. What about friends, however? Coworkers? You may not feel a moral responsibility to forge strong relationships with those people, but when you do, you find yourself more inclined to work on maintaining it.

When you think of how you relate to the people you named above, what are the traits that connected you?

_____

_____

_____

_____

_____

How many of them began by working together?

_____

Where we choose to work can be the common ground we share with others. Though you met at work, you share common passions and traits that create a bond. With those you listed above, the journey of your relationship was probably fairly easy. Imagine, if you could, developing a healthy relationship with nearly everyone you work with. How would your work days feel? Think about it. You go to work, and every person you communicate with is on your positive relationship list. How does your day flow in comparison to not having those connections?

As you consider this, take a moment to express how your work day feels when you have a positive relationship with everyone around you.

_____

_____

_____

_____

Sound unbelievable? It shouldn't. Sometimes the biggest divider when it comes to forging a relationship with a teammate is understanding how to communicate in a way that they feel valued and appreciated. When people feel valued, they become even better teammates. Perhaps you feel that unless you are a manager or leader in the workplace, it's not your responsibility to make others feel this way. But what would happen if you made it your responsibility? How?

Start with the understanding that not everyone communicates the same way. If you consider Gary Chapman's *The 5 Love Languages* (Chapman 1995), then the primary ways people show, and receive, appreciation are:

- Words of affirmation
- Touch
- Time
- Deeds
- Gifts

Understanding this context, love is defined as having an appreciation or concern for another. Begin to open your mind to the idea of focusing on speaking to others in their language rather than what yours may be naturally. Where to begin?

If you don't already have an understanding of how to recognize the different languages in action, let's start there.

Words of Affirmation: Hearing positive, specific words that bring value to the other person. Acknowledging their efforts with words.

Touch: A friendly hug or shoulder tap; acts that connect them to others.

Time: Giving moments to them, time focused on what matters to them.

Deeds: Completing tasks, or acts of service, without request.

Gifts: Receiving something that shows thoughtfulness toward them.

If you are someone who understands love through deeds, and someone is constantly trying to tell you how much they appreciate you, it will not resonate with you. The irony is that when you want to express to that very person your appreciation, you likely handle a task for them without being asked. You feel good about the fact that you expressed your care for them. Why didn't they acknowledge it? You're speaking different languages! How someone naturally communicates to you is how they best receive communication.

This one took me a while to grasp. For me, gifts is what came naturally, first and foremost. I would bring food, pick up a drink for someone, or provide some act of service like that. Even though I would feel good about my giving, it didn't resonate with everyone. Through deliberate practice, I found speaking through the other languages wasn't so difficult. As a matter of fact, as I thought about how to speak through the other vehicles of communication, I began to recognize where those very people had extended such acts toward me. That is when I finally began to understand. In order to speak to a teammate in a way for them to best receive my love, I needed to speak to them in the way they spoke to me. As I adjusted to being more thoughtful, the response to my efforts became more evident. My relationships became better understood and stronger.

Though gifts had been my primary language, I found myself better understanding the other four. When someone wants to hug me, I now understand what that means. I value it. When another asks what is on my mind, I take pause to appreciate their language of Time. No one has to make an effort, but when you choose to, you'll find it will be returned, in favor, most of the time.

Of the five languages listed above, which do you believe is your primary language?

As you think about the other languages, how might you adjust your message to deliver it in a different way that will resonate better with others?

_____

_____

_____

_____

_____

Relationships rule. In every one that I have been blessed to have, I grow and become a better version of myself. Whom do you become?

CHAPTER 15

WHAT DO YOU WANT TO BE REMEMBERED FOR?

By the time I was in my early twenties, I was already a divorced mother with a bustling career. My role had me on the road opening jewelry stores all over the state of Texas. Though my region was Northeast Texas, it wasn't uncommon for me to be in Central, West, or South Texas to help another supervisor. The areas I needed to frequent were not conveniently located to fly to, so I drove. If you have ever driven in Texas, you realize how far it is to drive north to south, not to mention east to west. I was logging around seven thousand miles a month for work. I don't know how I did it, but I managed to have only a total of two to four nights away from my son a month, and I made it a point to be home to tuck him into bed at night.

When you're juggling so many priorities, being organized is a must. In my early twenties I lacked true organization, so when a FranklinCovey time management class was being offered by my company, I jumped on it. My regional vice president, Rose, had gotten certified to teach the class, and when she stood in front of us her first question struck me: "What do you think people will remember about you when you pass?"

I wasn't expecting that question to launch a time management class. She went on to ask us what we would do if we had the luxury of an extra thirty minutes in our day. The questions layered, and of course it tied back to prioritizing your day by what is most important. If you have ever attended a time management class, they can be some of the longest days of your life. For me, I was blessed that Rose was teaching it; time with her always flew by.

When the class wrapped up, and I left to check in on my stores, her question came back to me: "What do you think people will remember about you when you pass?"

I hadn't given much thought to myself. I really didn't know. Being Mom to Jordan and senior partner to the twelve teams I supervised were what I gave most of my attention to. Even though I occasionally went out with a girlfriend, this might equate to a few hours every couple of weeks. So, what would people remember about me? I had no idea, and I hated not knowing. I began to reach out to my family and close friends to find out.

If you called those close to you and asked them what would they remember about you, what would they say?

_____

_____

_____

_____

_____

I made my calls and asked the question. I could hear the pause on the other end of the line. "Tanya, I'd remember how hard you work, how committed you are to your goals, and that you're a good mom."

Nearly every call I made was met with almost the same answer: I work hard, I'm committed, and I'm a good mom. Wow. This didn't feel good to hear even though the loved ones that said them to me believed them to be complimentary. A good mom? I wanted to be remembered as a *great* mom, and I definitely didn't want it to be an afterthought to my career. How could this be how they see me?

I didn't sleep that night, at least not well. I laid there thinking about the end of my life and what I would want to be remembered for. As morbid as it sounds, I visualized my loved ones and friends gathered around. When my eulogy was read, how would I want them to remember me? I knew I wanted my son, Jordan, to be the greatest accomplishment of my life, and he was.

Though a toddler at the time, I knew he would grow up to be a great man. I wanted to instill in him the unconditional love I have for him so he could love others in the same way. I wanted to shelter him from life and be sure he had every resource possible to achieve whatever he wanted. Being Jordan's mom and having him look up to me and appreciate the love and values I would instill in him was what I wanted people to recall about me. What else would I want to remembered for besides being a great mom to Jordan?

I wanted to be remembered for being there for others. If my family called or a friend needed me, I would make it a priority. They all knew how much and how hard I worked. So, if someone I cared about called and needed me, they would come before work. It was so rare that such calls would come, but truth be told, if I were working, I would let it go to voicemail, committing to myself that I would call them back after I was through working for the day. It was in this moment, the time that I was trying to decide how I wanted to be remembered, that I realized why such calls were so rare. It was because they knew they would get voicemail, so why bother? Sadness came over me. I get it. I see why they all led their answer with how hard I worked and such. It was because work had consumed my life. I made a decision that I would change.

I had decided two things I wanted to be remembered for, but what about a third? I'm not quite sure why I was focused on three, but I think Rose had mentioned something about three things when she expanded on her opening question. So, I came to these: 1) Tanya was a great mom to Jordan; he was her great accomplishment, and the love she had for him never wavered. 2) Tanya was a wonderful daughter/sister/aunt/friend. If you ever called her, she was there. She was also fiercely loyal. 3) Yes, but what about three?

This took me a bit longer, and it was about work, to some degree. I had worked really hard to earn the right to hold the role I was in. I had even gone through the pains of having to train not one, but two, different people to be my direct supervisor, as they had no working knowledge of the company's systems, processes, or culture (they were hired from outside the organization—a true Buy High, as written about earlier in this book). When the time came that I was promoted to senior partner, I felt I finally had a success I could appreciate, so I could take a breath. As I lay there trying to decipher how I wanted to be remembered when it came to work, it was complicated. Even though I had the title for the role I had been seeking, I didn't want that to be the memory. As I thought about it, the faces of all the people I had hired came to me. They were smiling and warm, welcoming. I loved those I had brought on board, and when they chose to join my team, I had a responsibility to them and their families to help them be as successful as they can be. The third thing I wanted to be remembered for, I finally decided, was honoring my commitment to the people that chose to work with me.

I ended up dozing off at some point, and when I woke up, I recalled the points I wanted to be known for. Rather than waiting until I'm dead, I can work toward being seen this way *now*. I made notes of my priorities, those three things, in my brand new FranklinCovey planner:

* **Jordan**: his well-being, and teaching him how to be a great person.
* **Family/friends**: they matter more than work. Answer the call. Be there.
* **Support those I hire**: commit to their growth and success.

As I woke Jordan to get ready for day care, I was full of happiness. Even though I hadn't slept, I felt alive. I felt I had focused my life on what matters to me, and there was no doubt I would recall the priorities when they were challenged by distractions. Jordan stretched, his curly red hair fluffy from his bath the night before, and he gave me a hug and kiss good morning. Life was good.

What three things do you want to be remembered for?

_____

_____

_____

_____

_____

Though that training class was held more than seventeen years ago, my values today still align with what I decided back then. Sure, they have expanded. Jordan is now twenty-one years old and figuring out his future. My family and friends know my work schedule, so when they call during my work day, I answer. With every person that I have hired or inherited from previous leadership, I find the things that matter to them lean into their goals and careers. I have better clarity of how to be the person I want to be and how to live the life God intended for me.

Even as I write this chapter, I am on a flight to Washington, DC, because my aunt passed away. She was more than an aunt to me. She was my godmother and my mom's best friend. My dad called in the middle of my work day, and when I saw his number on the screen, I called back immediately. He shared with me that she had passed away. It wasn't expected, and my parents were going to begin the drive to Richmond. I booked my flight.

Work? I hesitated to share the information with my leaders, only because most were off that day. When I sent an email to let them know, that I would need to make arrangements to be there, the outpouring of support they showed blessed me. They offered to work my shifts and pick up the slack of my absence, all without a moment's notice. Though guilt began to creep in because I am not one to put my responsibilities on others, they made it clear there was no guilt to be had. My mother needed me, and as I had promised to myself more than twenty years ago, I was on my way. Even as I lay down last night, one of my leaders sent a text asking me to be safe, reiterating that my presence would bring my mom comfort. He was right.

I don't share this to bring sadness. I hope it gives you some perspective on how guiding principles can help you see what is most important and, through that, how to be your best. Work made the third priority on my list, but this doesn't mean I don't work as hard as I did when I believed it was my number one. I still put in more hours than any of my leaders, and I am constantly finding ways to support them and the team. Just as when Rose asked us that simple question and I was motivated to set my course, I hope that as you read these words you are encouraged to define the principles you wish to live by.

If you're moved to begin the journey to lay out your road map for life with your principles as your navigator, jot the thoughts that are coming up for you, right now, so you don't lose them.

_____

_____

_____

_____

_____

Thanks for joining me on this journey called life.

If I've inspired you in any way, reach out to me on Facebook, Instagram, or other social media to ask any question you'd like. I'd love to share more and coach you along your journey. In the meantime, get out there and invest in others, get mentored yourself, and keep elevating your leadership skills each and every day.

"Be yourself, but always your better self."
—Karl G. Maeser

Dear Reader,

If you've gotten this far, it means (hopefully) that you have read this book, which was intended for you and me to meet through these words. If you are walking away with anything that has supported your personal growth, strengthened you as a leader, or motivated change in your company culture, then I consider this book a success.

Are you reading this while flying on a plane? Perhaps you are preparing to go to sleep for the night? Wherever you are while reading these words, know that we are connected. I hope you have a sense of my appreciation to share this space with you.

I did not set out to write a book. I didn't grow up wanting to be an author. I grew up wanting to help others and to give back in a meaningful way with no expectations in return. Through the journey of living out God's plan for me, I was connected to Tammy Kling and her team, who encouraged me to put my lessons into words. Have you ever written a book? If you have, this may be an easy process for you. If you haven't, then I hope you can appreciate how much love I drew from within to allow myself to put my philosophies and principles on paper. Where to begin?

As I said, I didn't plan what and when to write. While I was driving, thoughts would come to me that I knew should be part of this project. Siri and I spoke often, adding notes in my phone to reference later. It seemed most of the times I was inspired to write, I was afforded time to be in my own presence and able to shut out the world around me. I poured into these pages what was on my heart in regards to the topic at hand. The very first chapter I wrote was "My Favorite 'F' Word." The way to articulate it came flowing through me, and I couldn't wait to share it with Tammy and Tiarra, who supported me throughout the process.

I found the process of writing to be inspiring. I thought about you, the person who would look to my pages for learning. I wrote as though you were sitting in front of me, and we were having a conversation around the topic.

While on a plane back to Dallas, it hit me to design the book to be one that not only provoked thought but also encouraged you to write down your thoughts. Have you ever been inspired and then were unable to recall the thoughts that came up during your inspiration? I didn't want that to happen to you on this journey. Even more, I want you to be able to revisit your notes whenever needed. The notes you jotted down as you read this book will help you implement even more growth, whether for yourself or others.

You are important. You are unique, and your ability to be who you want to be is only limited by your scope of vision. You noticed I said who you want to be and not what you want to be. Of all the messages you walk away with, I hope the strongest is that who you are is what creates a legacy and fulfills larger meaning. What you choose to do with who you are is simply a way to share yourself. Don't be defined by what your professional role is. Expanding yourself will, as a wonderful side effect, improve your performance and results in what you do.

Thank you for spending your precious time with me. I hope you found it well spent, and, if so, please encourage others to walk this journey with me. The more people we can get focused on who they are, why they make the choices they do, and how it all connects, the better place our world becomes.

With gratitude and appreciation,
Tanya Waymire, A.C.C.
Erickson Certified Professional Coach
Member of the International Coach Federation

REFERENCE PAGE:

The triple bottom line – www.economist.com/node/14301663

Five Love Languages, by Gary Chapman
www.5lovelanguages.com

The Servant: A Simple Story About the True Essence of
Leadership, by James C. Hunter

Words are Currency, by Tammy Kling – www.onfirebooks.com